Marijuana New School

Outdoor Cultivation

A Reference
Manual with
Step-by-Step
Instructions

Marijuana New School
Outdoor Cultivation
Jeff Mowta

**A Reference
Manual with
Step-by-Step
Instructions**

Green Candy Press

Published by Green Candy Press
San Francisco, CA
www.greencandypress.com
ISBN 10: 1-931160-43-0
ISBN 13: 978-1-931160-43-8

Marijuana New School Outdoor Cultivation: A Reference Manual with Step-by-Step Instructions, by Jeff Mowta.

Printed in the U.S.A. by Publishers Express Press.
Sometimes massively distributed by P.G.W.

This book contains information about illegal substances specifically the plant Cannabis Sativa and its derivative products. Green Candy Press would like to emphasize that cannabis is a controlled substance in North America and throughout much of the world. As such, the use and cultivation of cannabis can carry heavy penalties that may threaten an individual's liberty and livelihood.

The aim of the Publisher is to educate and entertain. Whatever the Publisher's view on the validity of current legislation, we do not in any way condone the use of prohibited substances.

Contents

1

Growing with Seeds

The Starter Room

This section is about closet growing with regard to using minimal space to start young plants, using fluorescent or halide lights for raising seedlings, or for growing mother plants that will be used for cloning. This method of starting seedlings indoors requires little space and it is advantageous, even though this manual is about outdoor growing.

Fluorescent Closet System

The advantage of fluorescent lights, especially Envirolites®, is that they don't generate too much heat, which means that a grower can get away with using the following materials.

Materials

1. Fluoresecent lights (tubes or Envirolites®). Requirements: if tubes are used, they should fit in the desired space. If Envirolites® are used, one 95-watt bulb is used for every 2.6 square feet of growing space for vegetative growth and mother plants.

2. A custom gardening system for the desired space (chapter 3 has complete parts and instructions for building a system for any room size). The flood and drain system is the best for seedlings.

3. Smell removal system (if necessary); smell removal systems in the grow room are ionizers and air neutralizing agents such as Ona®.

Climate Maintenance

It is important to maintain a proper room temperature (70 to 80°F), a proper root temperature (slightly under 70°F), and a proper humidity (40 to 70%) so that the walls will not mold and plants are in a healthy environment for optimal growth.

Halide Closet-Size Unlimited System
Materials

1. 400 to 1,000-watt metal halide / sodium lights in a closet. A stationary 400-watt bulb effectively covers up to 16 square feet of space. Using a light mover adds another one-third of usable space, resulting in about 21 square feet. A stationary 1,000-watt bulb effectively covers up to 64 square feet. A track or Sun Circle® adds another one-third of usable square footage.
2. Oscillating fan.
3. Exhaust fan.
4. Air-cooling for lights (if necessary).
5. A custom gardening system for the desired space (see chapter 3).
6. Smell removal system (if necessary); smell removal systems in the grow room are ionizers and air neutralizing agents such as Ona®. For exhausting odors in the exhaust pipe, charcoal filters and ozone generators are used.

Maintenance

It is important to maintain a proper room temperature (70 to 80°F), a proper root temperature (slightly under 70°F), and a proper humidity (40 to 70%) so that the walls will not mold and plants are in a healthy environment for optimal growth.

In other words, the space may require good ventilation, air-cooled lights, and / or an air conditioner in order to acquire the proper variables for optimum or satisfactory growth if a grower uses the more powerful 400 to 1,000-watt halide / sodium bulbs.

In most cases, seedlings do not smell, but there are exceptions. For small spaces, an ionizer in the room should do the trick. For large areas where some odors escape from exhausting, a device to remove smell can be inserted into the exhaust pipe after the exhaust fan. For example, boxes with charcoal filters or ozone generators can be used to zap unwanted skunk-like odors before they are sent outside. There are ready-made products, such as Magic Dragon® and Uvonair® that can be inserted easily into exhaust pipes.

Seeds are placed in wet cloth.

Starting Seeds

Ideally, the grower cultivates with a strain (or many) that will grow well outdoors in the geographical area, produce a hearty yield, and have the odor and / or flavor of preference. It helps to know a seed's history. The more that is known, the less the gamble.

After obtaining the preferred seed stock, a grower should follow the next set of instructions in order to get off to a good start.

A. Water should be boiled (to sterilize), placed into a clean jar or glass, and allowed to cool to room temperature. Soaking the seeds in water for 24 to 48 hours is the next step. Then, seeds should be removed from the water and wrapped in wet cheesecloth or cotton. The seeds must not dry out. Lukewarm water can be used to remoisten the cloth.

B. A grower should find the sprouted germinants. Some germinants may sprout right away, while others may sprout days later.

C. The germinants should be placed into a growing medium. For the growing

New life. Seeds have germinated.

medium, a grower has several choices, such as potting soil, soilless mix, peat moss, rockwool cubes, oasis cubes, or peat pellets. Before seeds are placed in medium, a small hole should be made to bury the seedling so that it lies ⅛ to ¼ inches under the medium. The seed part should be up, and the white tail should be pointing downward. The seedling should be handled delicately when it is covered in the medium so that the stalk does not break.

1. Sprouted seeds can be put in pots (about 4 inches high) that contain potting soil, soilless mix, or peat moss. Several germinants can be placed in one container at first, then they should be transplanted into individual containers before they start to develop too many roots. Normally, less than a week is a good amount of time to wait before transplanting the young plants into individual containers. After a week or so, roots will tangle and the job becomes more difficult. The longer the wait before putting a germinant in its own container, the greater the odds of stunting the plant. A spoon can be used to scoop out tiny plants so that they can be moved to individual containers.

2. For rockwool or oasis cubes, seedlings again should be put in the medium with the tail pointing down. Cubes must not be allowed to dry out. If cubes dry out, plants can die or growth can be stunted.

3. Peat pellets work too. In order to use peat pellets, water must be added to the cubes, which will make the cubes expand. When the cubes expand, the germinants can be buried in the peat pellets with the white tail pointing downward.

D. The seedlings should be placed 1 to 3 inches beneath fluorescent lights or 1½ to 2 feet beneath a 400-watt metal halide bulb.

Often the more expensive specialty fluorescent grow tubes are worth the extra bucks. Daylight fluorescent tubes work too. Alternating a cool white and a warm white in a fluorescent light fixture is a cheap way of making it through the seedling phase. Using only cool whites or warm whites will work, if no other tubes are available, but using only warm whites or only cool whites results in slower growth and some plants may turn a little yellow due to inadequate lighting.

Mice
Mice like to eat fresh, young shoots. Therefore, they should not have access to young plants.

Seedling Care
Feeding
A fertilizing routine should be started a couple of weeks after germination. A grower should use fertilizer only at half strength during vegetative growth. An example is to use Sea Mix™ 3-2-2, Alaska Fish Fertilizer ®, or liquid kelp at the recommended rate. It may be easiest to use only one fertilizer for all feedings, unless the grower is confident about combining fertilizers.

If plants are placed on a flood table, feeding maintenance is lowered dramatically. A leak-proof table can be flooded periodically by hand or a pump. Pumps are convenient for lots of plants. Chapter 3 explains how to build a flood and drain system.

Overwatering and underwatering can stunt a plant, which leads to poor production. Overwatering is most common in potting soil that is not allowed to drain. When potting soil is saturated with water, there is little air in the soil. When cubes or soilless mix are frequently saturated with solution, the solution drains well and the roots can receive an abundance of air due to the nature of the medium.

Seedlings that are severely yellow, with stiff, woodlike stalks will not grow to be healthy plants. They will be stunted. The stalks should be soft and bendable.

One option is to mist the plants daily or every few days with a sprayer.

Lighting

If fluorescent lights are used, each pot should be placed so that the top is $\frac{1}{2}$ to 2 inches beneath tubes.

For a 400-watt halide light, the light distance should start at 1 $\frac{1}{2}$ to 2 feet above the plants.

As the plants grow, the lights should be raised so they are always at a constant distance from the plant tops to avoid burns.

Running the lights for 18 hours on a timer is recommended during vegetative growth. However, keeping the lights on for 24 hours with no timer is another possibility that works.

Temperature

Seedlings can grow well in cool and warm temperatures, however hot temperatures can stunt plants. The ability to grow well in cool temperatures varies from strain to strain. A temperature around 70 to 80°F is safe for most strains.

Moving Seedlings Outdoors

After seedlings are one month old and there is little risk of frost, they can be transplanted to an outdoor system (site) or a greenhouse or cheap coldframe. Good glass can make better light!

Plants can moved out of a seedling room sooner (after 2 to 3 weeks), but the growth rate will be slow until the plants are about 6 weeks old, and they will be more vulnerable to predators, such as mice and slugs. When growing outdoors, seedlings can go into some kind of outdoor mini-greenhouse (cold frame) in early spring, soon before or after the last day of frost, if rainy conditions are not dominating. If the weather is terrible and growth is spindly, transplanting seedlings into larger containers and burying them up to their first set of leaves

These seedlings are getting a good start with natural sunlight.

may prevent a disaster. Roots will grow from the stalk, and the plants will recover from their weak state.

Some young plants can fight off adverse weather, such as frosts, if the strain has the potential in its genes.

If a mini-greenhouse is used for outdoor cultivation, there are several possible types. The options are pretty much endless, but, a simple rule is to keep the plants covered with 6ml clear plastic. Adding an exhaust fan is recommended if the grow zone is not temporary.

Plants in the Northern Hemisphere (above the Tropic of Cancer) are normally transplanted after March 22 when the days are getting longer. (September 22 is the ordinary date for the Southern Hemisphere.)

Building a Hoophouse
Tools
1. Handsaw.
2. Hammer.
3. Exacto knife.
4. Shovel (if corner posts are dug into the ground).

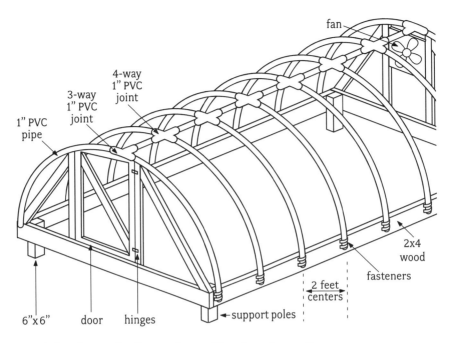

fan

4-way
1" PVC
joint

3-way
1" PVC
joint

1" PVC
pipe

2x4
wood

fasteners

2 feet
centers

6"x 6"   door   hinges   ←support poles

Simple hoophouse plan for starting seedlings in cooler weather.

Materials

1. One-inch PVC pipe (10 to 12-foot lengths); two pieces for every 2 feet of hoop-house length.
2. 2x4 wood for bottom frame.
3. 3 to 3 ½-inch wood nails.
4. 6x6-inch posts for the corners of the frame.
5. Door.
6. In-line fan.
7. 6ml clear poly (greenhouse grade preferred).
8. Fasteners for mounting the 1-inch PVC against the 2x4.
9. Four-way 1-inch PVC joints, one for every two pieces of 1-inch PVC pipe in the frame, minus the first and last fittings which will be 3-way 1-inch PVC joints.
10. Two 3-way 1-inch PVC joints.
11. Two 1-foot lengths of 1-inch PVC.
12. In-line fan and matching 2 to 4-foot length of stovepipe.

Procedure

A. The four corner posts should be cut to equal lengths and buried in the ground, or placed on flat hard ground like cement.

B. 2x4s are hammered with nails to the posts in order to make a rectangle box.

C. Now, the center spine is made.
    1. At the front end there is a 3-way joint.
    2. Then a 2-foot length is connected, followed by 4-way joints.
    3. The pattern is repeated until the last 3-way joint is connected to the last 2-foot length. For extra strength, all connections can be glued with PVC glue.

D. The first 2 pieces of the long 1-inch PVC pipe should be inserted into the first 3-way fitting, then clamped to the side 2x4s. The next step is to repeat this for all of the long pipes.

E. The house can be covered with a sheet of 6ml plastic.

Smart Option
An in-line fan and a 2 to 4-foot piece of stovepipe can be hung inside of the house and a small hole can be cut in the rear of the hoophouse for air to exhaust.

To maintain a top-quality environment, cooling or heating a greenhouse are options.

Heating a Greenhouse

A greenhouse can be heated with the following systems. Glass holds warm air in a greenhouse better than other materials.
1. Unit heater such as a forced-air heater (good for small greenhouses).
2. Convection tubes.
3. Central heating (uses hot water or steam). Good method on big-scale.
4. Radiant heaters (heats the area near plants, not all of the air).
5. Solar heat. This stores heat in a collector, and can be used with a backup heating source that activates when this system is not sufficient.

Cooling a Greenhouse
A greenhouse can be cooled with the following items.
1. A roof vent allows hot air to leave a greenhouse in a mild climate. In a hot climate, this will not be sufficient.
2. Shade cloth can be used to cover the roof and ⅔ of the sides of the greenhouse. These come in shades that block out light at 30%, 40%, 50%, 60%, and 70%. The right strain should be used with shade cloth.
3. Evaporative cooling (heat exchangers). These can cool temperatures under hot conditions. They can be used with shade cloth, too. This will save energy.

Transplanting Seedlings
Plants can be transplanted at any time of the vegetative growth phase. As a general rule, plants should be able to spread their roots and not become too root-bound. Plants should not be transplanted during budding.

Plants can be transplanted from one medium to another. For example, plants in rockwool, clay, perlite, soilless mix or dirt can go into any other medium.

Plant roots will adapt to various root environments. The key is to feed the roots properly at all times. For example, a plant in peat moss or soilless mix that is transplanted to clay or perlite will need a new feeding program because soilless mix can be constantly irrigated or it can go days between irrigation. However, roots located in a medium such as clay cannot go days between waterings, given that plants are grown under a strong climate.

For hydroponic growing, following a pattern of continuous feeding for 6 days and flushing for 1 to 2 days is the safest method for providing a healthy root environment for the plants in all hydroponic mediums.

When plants are transplanted from a hydroponic medium into soil, the plants can be cared for as though they are being grown in soil. Plants should be transplanted from a hydroponic (aeroponic) medium into soil at the youngest age possible in order to prevent stress.

Roots in soil or soilless mix anchor in the medium to keep roots intact. That makes transplanting a snap, especially if mix is neither too wet nor too dry. A grower should always keep soilless mix somewhere between too dry and too wet if feeding is done periodically (i.e. once a week). However, plants grown in soilless mix that are continuously fed with a top-feeding hydroponic system will grow faster than plants that are fed or watered periodically in soilless mix.

Outdoor gardening systems can be put together several ways, using systems such as soil / soilless, hydroponic, and aeroponic. Systems and feeding instructions are discussed in full detail in chapter 3.

Plants can be spaced far from each other and left to grow together, or they can be put closer together and trained away from each other.

Outdoor container plants using soil / soilless mix can have up to 3 seedlings per 5 to 20-gallon container.

What a Grower Should Know about Seedlings

Pulling plants with male sex characteristics (males and hermaphrodites) allows for the production of seedless buds. In order to make seeds, identifying and using pollen immediately (or storing immediately in the freezer) is the key, especially for the serious breeder. Breeding is explained in detail in chapter 6.

Marijuana plants are male, female, or both (hermaphrodites). When a grower knows the difference he can make the garden grow more efficiently by, for instance, growing only female buds.

Sexing Seedlings

Some growers can identify the sex of plant seeds.

A trick to sexing plants that are 3 to 5 weeks old is to decrease the photoperiod from 18 hours to 12. When the lights run at 12 hours for 3 to 5 days, the plants' flowering mechanisms are triggered. After the 3 to 5 days, the light timer should be reset to run for 18 hours. In most cases, males show their forming pollen sacks in a week, give or take a couple of days, while females normally show their pistils soon afterwards. Sometimes, though, a female will show pistils sooner than a male shows pollen.

Putting Seedlings through the Test

Putting young seedlings through tests such as overwatering, underwatering, drought, high heat, low light, coldwater-feeding, or crowding can help sort out the strong plants from the weak. Testing can also allow a grower to have the genetics that a plant needs in order to survive in a particular climate.

However, just because plants look best at a young age does not mean that they will necessarily demonstrate the ability to outproduce those that were shocked or died at a young age due to adverse conditions. Nevertheless, plants that are strong in youth tend to continue being strong plants through adulthood.

2

Growing
with Clones

Cloning is fairly easy and should be done when plants are in vegetative growth. Cloning involves taking a piece of a known mother plant and creating other plants with the same genetic makeup. A mother plant should be a vigorous, healthy female plant with plenty of shoots to take cuttings from.

When clones are taken in vegetative growth and rooted, they will grow quickly right off the bat. This is a good habit to get into for cutting clones.

Clones taken from plants that don't show any flowers (i.e. 2 weeks into budding) may produce small buds during the 18 hour rooting photoperiod. However, they rejuvenate into vegetative growth rather quickly when they are put in a vegetative light cycle or long daylight days after they form roots.

Plants that are cloned during the flowering process (when buds are noticeable) will take longer to revert into fast vegetative growth and time is lost. Sometimes, depending on many factors such as the strain, plants will not revert to healthy vegetative growth. This means that plants will take on a permanent one to four leaf growth pattern, and they will not be as compact as they would if they had a regular leaf pattern of five, seven, or nine leaves. The plants will be far less productive than clones taken during vegetative growth.

The stage of the budding process at which the clones are taken has a big impact on the quality of the new cuttings' growth. Clones taken toward the end of the budding process have more potential problems than those taken earlier in the budding process. Checking leaf texture also helps in determining plant quality. If the leaves of the new cuttings become waxy and stiff, unlike normal soft and flexible growth, then problems can be expected. Plants with the waxy material should be pulled, because they will be unproductive. Plants with an abnormal leaf pattern but normal-textured leaves will probably rejuvenate to become productive.

Plants That Are Started from Seed

When seed is used for growing outdoors, a grower has the option of cutting female clones when the plant sex is determined. The female sex can be determined by finding pistils growing from the nodes (stalk and branch intersections). Looking for early flower formations is advised, too. Extreme emphasis must be placed on the importance of this knowledge. Plants with the pistils should not have male pollen sacks along the stalks. Those plants that have pollen and pistils are hermaphrodites, and these plants can make an unknown quantity of seed.

Hermaphroditism can creep in at any time, although it occurs very rarely, especially in a quality garden.

Cloning Supplies

1. 10x20-inch tray and matching propagation lid (7 inches high).
2. Propagation mat or heat pad.
3. Thirty or more $1\frac{1}{2}$-inch Oasis propagation cubes, rockwool cubes or small plastic cutting containers.
4. Vitamin B_1 1.7oz (50ml).
5. Rooting hormone.
6. Fluorescent light fixture with bulbs, or Envirolites®.
7. Timer (optional).

Cloning Procedure

A. 4 to 6 shoots should be left above the spot where the cut is made. This is a critical step. The new cutting-to-be will have about 3 shoots at the top and 2 more down the stalk.

B. The next step is removing 2 bottom side shoots. Different strains will have different growth patterns of the spaces between the node intersections. It is best to have a cutting in which both cut nodes can fit into the rooting medium.

C. Next, the cutting should be placed in a jar of water. The procedure is repeated until the desired number of cuttings has been taken. It is better for a novice to take only a few cuttings at a time, so that the learning curve will be faster. There is no point in taking 30 cuttings, only to find that one mistake (e.g., drying out the rooting medium) ruined the whole batch.

D. The next step is soaking Oasis cubes (organic), rockwool cubes (not organic), or cutting containers with a fresh soilless mix like Sunshine® #2 mix, Jiffy Mix, or Pro Mix. Oasis cubes and rockwool are simpler for the novice. A recommended organic method is soaking rooting medium in a liquid mixture. For instance, in 1-gallon of water add ½ the recommended strength of liquid kelp and a few drops of Vitamin B_1. Alternatively, a few drops of Vitamin B_1 works well on its own. Some people use only plain water and get high survival.

E. Now excess water should be squeezed out of the growing medium. Too much water, and the rooting process becomes slower. If the rooting medium is too dry, the cuttings can wilt and die. Wet, but not too wet, is the way to get decent results. Some say that if the rooting medium is not too wet, the cuttings form new roots more quickly, because the plant will tend to seek out water by spreading its roots. However, this is a fine line because too little water will be severely detrimental to the cuttings' chances of survival.

F. A nail can be used to make holes in the cubes or growing mix, if no holes are present. The hole should not go all of the way through the cloning medium. The 2 side-shoot nodes should be covered by the cloning medium without the stem going through the bottom.

G. The bottom 2 nodes of the cutting are dipped into a rooting hormone, then placed in the cubes or containers. This procedure is repeated for all the cuttings.
    If the distances between the cut nodes are too far apart to be covered by the rooting cubes, then an option is to stack a cube on top of another cube. If soilless mix— perlite, vermiculite, etc.—is used, then a deeper container will solve the depth problem.

H. The clones are then placed in a tray and covered with the lid (a piece of clear, raised plastic designed to fit the tray). The tray can be placed on a propagating mat, or 1-inch above a heating pad, especially if the clones are rooting in a cold area. Clones will root faster when the roots receive proper heat (approximately 70°F). If clones are rooting at room temperature, the roots in the medium will be cooler than room temperature.

I. Fluorescent tubes should be placed 2 to 4 inches above dome (or Envirolites® at 2 feet above clones for every 4x4 area) to supply adequate lighting during rooting. The lights should be set on a timer to run for 18 hours a day. However, rooting clones under a 24 hour photoperiod does the trick. Nevertheless, it is a good idea to give the plants a 6 hour rest. It is natural for plants to take a night-cap since that is the world they are accustomed to.

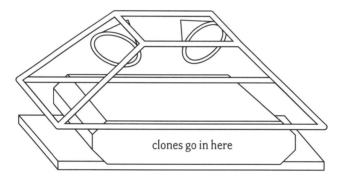

clones go in here

Typical cloning setup; tray, lights and heat pad.

Maintenance

The plastic lid should not have any cracks or warps because clones could dry up and die overnight, especially babied clones from a weak strain. However, some strains are more sensitive to a bad lid than others.

Some growers mist several times a day. This can give better results. Sometimes lids retain a lot of moisture; sometimes the moisture escapes easily from under the lid. Roots may start growing out of bottoms and sides of the cubes within 1 to 4 weeks. The time length varies from strain to strain.

Periodically adding small amounts of plain water to the cubes or mix is a good idea, especially if the medium seem gets a little dry. Oversoaking is wrong and is not going to help matters. Overwatering slows down the rooting process and can also cause stem rot. Overwatered clones that do make it are often weak and may not form a strong plant.

Some growers don't mist at all, leave their cuttings fully exposed to the air, and yet get decent results while believing that only the strong survive. However, this method causes the roots to use up a lot of water. Therefore, frequent watering to the roots is a must when moistening the roots with this method, or keeping the roots sitting in a shallow solution of water / nutrient solution. Less air is available to the roots with constant liquid saturation.

If rooting medium sits full-time in a solution of liquid, the cuttings will be slow rooters, and the cuttings will develop a skinnier network of roots, which will put the plant behind in terms of productivity.

Transplanting Clones

As soon as roots show from the cubes or mix, the clones should be transplanted into the desired bucket, such as 5-gallon containers.

Sometimes, if several clones are started at the same time, some may seem to root, while others look weak or dying. Weak-looking cuttings can be given a little tug so that a grower knows which cuttings are rooting and which ones aren't. The cuttings that resist have anchoring roots, while the really weak or dying clones will come out easily.

Transplanting Procedure

Plants can be transplanted at any time of the vegetative growth phase. As a general rule, plants should be able to spread their roots and not become too root-bound. Plants should not be transplanted during flowering.

Plants can be transplanted from one medium to another. For example, plants in rockwool, clay, perlite, soilless mix, or dirt can go into any other medium.

Plant roots will adapt to various root environments. The key is to feed the roots properly at all times. For example, a plant in peat moss or soilless mix that is transplanted to clay or perlite will need a new feeding program, because soilless mix can be constantly irrigated or it can go days between irrigation. However, roots located in a medium such as clay cannot go days between waterings, given that plants are grown under a strong climate. The same holds true if a plant is transplanted from a medium like rockwool or clay into soil or soilless mix.

Roots in soil or soilless mix anchor in the medium to keep roots intact. That makes transplanting a snap, especially if the mix is neither too wet nor too dry. A grower should always keep soilless mix somewhere between too dry and too wet.

Cloning Outdoor Plants

Outdoor clones can be taken at any time before budding, but sooner is better for obtaining a large plant size.

Clones taken from budding plants will be less productive. Those cuttings have the potential for not reverting to vegetative growth, and may never grow healthily, which makes for poor production.

For example, two clones taken at the same time from two different flowering mothers may have two different responses. One may put on healthy vegetative mass with the proper photoperiod, while the other may flower under the same photoperiod and produce low-productive buds. Both plants will grow slowly at first, whether they continue to bud or put on vegetative growth.

Cloning budding plants is not recommended, because the results are chancy, and such poor methodology is a waste of time if growing a productive, healthy crop is the desired result.

Rooting Clones for Outdoor Growing Using Natural Light

Cuttings may be taken from mother plants that are growing indoors or outdoors. The procedure for preparing cubes or mix is the same as described earlier in this chapter, except they are placed outdoors in a miniature sealed plastic (6ml) cold frame when the daylight hours are decent (approximately 16 hours) and days are getting longer. The Oasis cube, rockwool cube, or mix surrounding the cutting should be buried under dirt or site mix to keep the roots warm in cool weather or cool in hot weather.

For smooth rooting, a grower should check the rooting progress periodically and water the cubes or mix when they begin to dry out. Outdoor predators can damage a locale. For example, a nosy bear can leave holes all over a plastic hut.

3

Outdoor Cultivation Systems

Hydroponics
Building a Flood and Drain System
Flood Table Materials

1. Flood table made to size or plastic store-bought model.
2. Two ½-inch poly elbows.
3. Two ½-inch poly Ts.
4. One roll of ¾-inch tubing.
5. Two ¾-inch thru-hull fittings.
6. One reservoir (should hold about 12 gallons of fertilized solution per each 4x4 table space).
7. Plastic covering for tray, or a growing medium such as perlite, perlite / vermiculite, coco fibers / perlite, or expanded clay.
8. Pump (250 to 350 mag drive for 4x4 to 12x12 space. Stronger pumps can be used for larger tables.)
9. Panty hose to cover pump (optional).
10. ¾-inch plywood to support table.
11. Four sawhorse hinges per table.
12. Eight pieces of 2x4 cut to identical lengths for the legs. The table height should be slightly higher than the reservoir.
13. Two pieces of 2x4 for table support. These will connect two sets of legs.
14. ½-inch poly-threaded female fitting to attach to pump.
15. Intermittent timer.

Tools

1. Drill.
2. One-inch hole saw.
3. Saw.
4. Pipe wrench or crescent wrench.
5. Knife.

Setting Up the System

A. 2x4s should be cut to length so that when the sawhorse legs are set up, the reservoir will be slightly lower than the table. Each pair of sawhorse brackets will be joined with another 2x4 to give the table support.

B. Flood table is placed on the ¾-inch plywood.

Making a Homemade Flood Table

If wood is used to make a flood table, it should be ¾-inch plywood. Anything thinner will warp.

Once plywood is cut to size, 1x4-inch wood should be nailed to the sides. For simplicity, the following instructions assume that a 4x8-foot sheet of plywood is used for the table.

Two 8-foot lengths of 1x4-inch wood should be nailed to the long lengths of the plywood.

One 8-foot length of 1x4-inch wood that is cut in half can be used for the short sides; then the small sides are nailed together from the bottom of the plywood.

Caulking should be applied along the nailed seams for extra waterproofing.

The table should be placed on something that supports it. A quick sawhorse can be made with cheap 2x4-inch wood and with hinges that the 2x4-inch wood slides into. Another 2x4 (i.e. an eight footer for an 8 to 4-foot flood table) is placed between the hinges to complete an instant sawhorse. One end should be an inch or so higher than the other end so that the solution can be recirculated.

In the middles of the two widths, two holes should be made about 2 inches from the end of the table using a 1-inch hole saw. Diagram shows a table with tubing connected to thru-hull fittings underneath the table.

Now, two layers of 6ml black poly plastic should be used to cover the bottom and sides of the table.

The spots where the holes should be made will be obvious if the table is store-bought.

A thru-hull fitting is inserted into each hole. Extra care is needed in the homemade flood table: the plastic should be carefully drawn through the thru-hull fittings and the hole in the plywood by making a small hole in the 6ml plastic. When the thru-hull fitting goes through the table, black 6ml plastic should be seen tightly secured against the threads of the thru-hull fitting. Now the plastic can be cut out from underneath the table, and the female fastener can be used to tighten the thru-hull fitting to the flood table. Now the system will be leak-free. Care must be taken so that top layer of plastic does not get cut open. If the top plastic layer has a hole, water can leak into the bottom plastic layer. This will create a balloon-like effect from the trapped water. Cutting plastic away from the thru-hull fitting can prevent water from trapping between the plastic layers.

C. The pump is placed in the bottom of the reservoir and a ½-inch female fitting is attached to the pump.

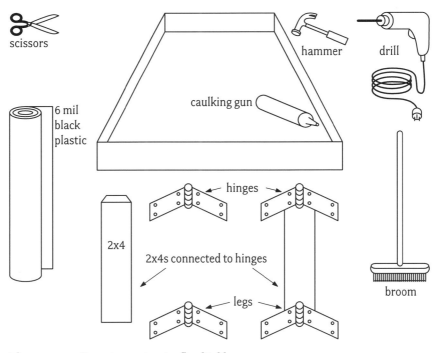

The necessary items to construct a flood table.

D. Two 4-inch pieces of ½-inch tubing are connected to the thru-hull fittings (for holes that are made at the ends of the tables). Heating the ½-inch tubing with hot water will make the connection easier. The next step is connecting two ½-inch elbows to the ½-inch tubing. Then, ½-inch black poly tubing is connected to each end of the elbows. When the two ends of the black poly tubing meet in the middle, a T-fitting should be inserted; this can be run to the pump.

E. The pump is connected to ½-inch tubing. Just above the pump, a piece of the ½-inch tubing should be cut out and a ½-inch T should be inserted. The exposed end of the T should be connected to ½-inch tubing and then to an *on/off* tap that will act as a bypass valve. Another piece of ½-inch black poly tubing can be connected to the end of the tap, followed by an elbow so that solution splashes and is aerated without making any mess.

Feeding
F. Method A (for small to large plants)
1 to 4-gallon containers (mesh pots) can be placed on the table and filled with soilless mix (such as Sunshine #2 mix). The plants should at first be top-fed continually (for fastest growth) or periodically (slower growth with a lot less maintenance) until the roots are visible at the bottom of the container.

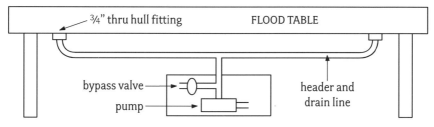

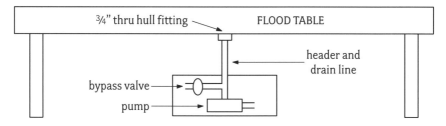

Side views of two slightly different flood table models.

When the roots are visible at the bottoms of the containers, a grower has two options.

1. Put a 1-inch layer of perlite on the table. The feeding intervals can be once a day or more often. One study done under identical growing conditions showed yields that were almost identical between one batch that was fed continually and the other batch that was fed in the morning. Perlite holds air and moisture with nutrients in between feedings.

2. Put a sheet of reflectix material on top of the flood table with holes cut to size to fit the containers. Reflectix will help keep the roots cooler. The reflectix can be used with or without perlite undernearth, but if there is no perlite, a grower should feed a few times a day. If perlite is used, one feeding a day is all that is required.

Method B (for midsize to large plants)
A custom-sized sheet of reflectix material is precut. This material will cover the table and will fit securely over each slab. The slabs are placed under the holes with a secure fit.

When the clones are ready for transplanting, they should be placed into the 1-foot rockwool slab. A grower should do the first couple of feedings from the top until the roots reach the bottom of the slab, or he could allow the table to flood lots of solution for the first couple of feedings.

Flooding and draining should be done several times a day at a water level over $\frac{1}{4}$-inch. Six or more floods at regular intervals should work. A timer is used to control the period for which the flooding takes place. The time depends on the flow rate and and size of the table. Using a wristwatch and a couple of manual floods will give a grower the amount of seconds that need to be programmed into the timer so that the solution fills the table to the desired level.

A little extra tip: most hydroponic feeding systems can be converted to aeroponic systems with a high-pressure pump, misters / feeder lines to mist the roots and / or leakproofing, if necessary.

Building a Custom Top-Feeding System
Option A: Flood Table

The advantage of using a flood table in a top-feeding system is that it is very cheap to make and it has less fittings than most other systems. Also, if a line accidentally comes out of a container the solution will leak on the table, rather than all over the floor.

A. A grower should buy or build a flood table and a stand to support the table for the prescribed growing area. For a small closet, a plastic flood table made to size may be hard to find. If wood is used to make a flood table, it should be sturdy, like ¾-inch plywood. For a small closet space, cutting a piece of plywood that leaves about 6 inches to each wall works in order to build a custom garden. For larger rooms, enough space should be left to walk around the tables and in between them (i.e. 1 to 2 feet between tables and walls).

Once plywood is cut to size, 1x4-inch wood should be nailed to the sides. For simplicity, this example will assume that a 4x8-foot sheet of plywood is used for the table.

Two 8-foot lengths of 1x4-inch wood should be nailed to the long lengths of the plywood.

One 8-foot length of 1x4-inch wood cut in half can be nailed to the short sides. The small sides are nailed together from the bottom of the plywood.

Caulking should be used as a waterproofing safety measure. Caulking is applied along the nailed seams.

Finally, black 6ml poly can be used to cover the wood table.

B. The table is placed on something that supports it. A quick sawhorse can be made with cheap 2x4-inch wood with hinges that the 2x4-inch wood slides into. Another 2x4 (i.e. an eight footer for an 8x4-foot flood table) is placed between the hinges to complete an instant sawhorse.

When a table is made, the sides furthest from the reservoir should be the highest and at equal height.

The sides nearest the reservoir should be an inch or so lower. One of the nearest sides near the reservoir should be slightly lower (i.e. 2 inches lower on an 8-foot table). The drain hole should be above the lowest corner.

C. In one corner of the flood table, a hole should be made using a 1-inch hole saw.

Homemade models: When using black poly plastic, the plastic should be cut away from the hole so that water will not get trapped in black poly layers. Then, a ¾-inch PVC pipe is connected to the reservoir to allow for draining.

Small, hidden buds are a good place to make seeds before pistils turn bronn.

F. A piece of ½-inch poly tubing is cut about the same length as the flood table.

G. A ½-inch end cap is inserted at the end of the table.

H. A ½-inch poly elbow is inserted at the other end that is nearest the reservoir. The elbow should be directly above the reservoir.

I. A piece of ½-inch black poly tubing should be connected to the other end of the elbow, and then connected to the pump. A highly recommended option is to put a bypass valve or a ½-inch T just after the pump so that the solution stays aerated and agitated, and the flow can be controlled. More ½-inch fittings can be placed on the bypass valve so that the aerated liquid is forced to the bottom near the pump. Also, forcing water downward can reduce possibilities of splashing and making a mess on the floor.

J. Mesh pots (2 to 5-gallon) can be placed on the table with the plants. Using larger containers is recommended for longer growing cycles. Any hydroponic medium can be used to grow the plants, such as clay, perlite, soilless mix, perlite / coconut fibers, or perlite / vermiculite.

K. Small holes should be inserted into the ½-inch poly header line that is on the flood table. A punch or small drill bit can be used to make the holes for the fittings.

L. ⅛ or ³⁄₁₆-inch tubing is connected to the fittings and each line is attached to each pot using alligator stakes. It is best to look ahead to see where the plants will be when it is harvest time so that the proper lengths will be cut.

M. When plant roots show out the bottoms of the containers, more hydroponic medium such as clay or perlite should be placed under the containers that are on the table so that the roots will be covered and aerated, or another mesh pot can be turned upside down and placed under the plants if duct tape is used to fasten them together. If the container sits on a flood table for too long, roots can turn brown from lack of oxygen.

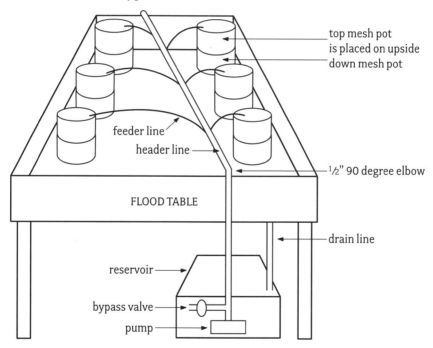

Top-feeding system utilizes buckets on a flood table.

Feeding
It is easiest to feed the plants with the pump timer running full-time only during the light hours. A solar pump would do this. But plants can be fed continuously (all day and all night). Also, plants can be fed intermittently (i.e. every 20 minutes for 2 minutes) during the light hours, or for all hours.

Option B: Bucket System

Tools

1. Drill and 1-inch hole saw.
2. Knife.
3. Wrench.

Materials

1. One 3 to 4-gallon mesh pot or one solid 3 to 4-gallon bucket per plant.
2. One 5-gallon bucket per plant.
3. One to two ¾-inch thru-hull fittings per plant (one for mesh pot, two for solid buckets).
4. One ¾-inch T per plant.
5. ¾-inch yellow flex hose (enough to connect plants together and to connect to reservoir).
6. One reservoir with ¾-inch thru-hull fitting in the bottom.
7. One ¾-inch T.
8. One roll of ½-inch black poly tubing.
9. One roll of ⅛ or ³⁄₁₆-inch black poly tubing.
10. One fitting per plant to connect ½-inch tubing to ⅛ or ³⁄₁₆-inch tubing.
11. One alligator stake per plant.
12. One ½-inch T fitting.
13. One ½-inch end cap.
14. One to two ½-inch elbows.
15. One ½-inch female threaded fitting for pump.
16. One pump.

Support System: Building the system

Plants grown in a bucket system in the closet do not need much time for vegetative growth before flowering. However, plants grown to the ceiling in a larger room will need more time to complete the whole cycle.

With a bucket system, a mesh pot or bucket (with plant and growing medium) is stacked into a 5 to 7-gallon pail.

A. If a bucket is used, a ¾-inch thru-hull fitting should be inserted into the bottom so that solution can drain into the bottom pail.

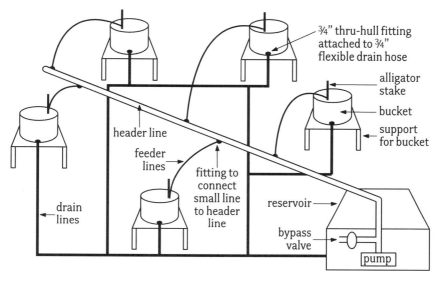

Assembled view of a top-feeding bucket system.

B. The bottom pail should have a ¾-inch thru-hull fitting in the side near the bottom. If this hole is too low, the thru-hull fitting won't fit.

C. A short piece (approximately 6 inches) of ¾-inch yellow hose should be attached to the ¾-inch thru-hull fitting.

D. A ¾-inch T should be inserted into the other end of the hose.

E. The open ends of the T should be connected to other buckets with yellow flex tubing.

F. After all buckets are connected, there should be two open ends from the ¾-inch T fittings attached to two of the buckets. The final stage is to attach these fittings to hose, then to attach both ends of hose to another ¾-inch T. Then the hose is connected to the ¾-inch thru-hull fitting on the bottom of the reservoir. The reservoir should be located lower than the pails so the pails drain well.

G. A piece of ½-inch poly tubing (feeder line) is cut and laid near the plants.

H. A ½-inch end cap is inserted at the end away from the reservoir. Soaking tubing in hot water allows for easier connections.

I. A ½-inch poly elbow is inserted at the open end that is nearest the reservoir. The elbow should be directly above the reservoir.

J. ½-inch black poly tubing should be connected to the other end of the elbow and then to the pump. A highly recommended option is to put a bypass valve or a ½-inch T just after the pump so that the solution stays aerated and agitated, and the flow can be controlled. More ½-inch fittings can be placed on the bypass valve so that the aerated liquid is forced to the bottom near the pump. Also, forcing water downward can reduce possibilities of splashing and making a mess on the floor.

K. Small holes should be poked into the ½-inch poly header line that is on the flood table. A punch or small drill bit can be used to make the holes for the fittings.

L. ⅛ or ³⁄₁₆-inch tubing is connected to the fittings and secured to each pot using alligator stakes. It is best to look ahead to see where the plants will be when it is harvest time so that the proper lengths can be cut.

Feeding
It is easiest to feed the plants with the pump timer running full-time only during the light hours. A solar pump would allow for this. But plants can be fed continuously (all day and all night). Also, plants can be fed intermittently (i.e. every 20 minutes for 2 minutes) during the light hours, or for all hours.

Hydroponic to Aeroponic Conversion
Many top-feeding hydroponic systems can be converted to aeroponic systems by using a stronger pump, adding a mister for each plant, and changing the position of the mister to feed roots in the air (under the lid) as opposed to top feeding. Hydroponic systems that use less growing medium will work best, such as those grown in PVC or gutter pipe.

In this case, a small, say, 6-inch mesh pot will be used to replace the old 3-gallon bucket. The mesh pot with a small amount of growing medium should then be placed in a lid. Then the mesh pot gets inserted into a 5 to 7-gallon pail.

Adding a mister for each bucket (to feed inside the pail) and a high-powered pump completes the conversion. A small hole must be made in the 5 to 7-gallon pail to accomodate the tubing and mister. ⅛ to ¼-inch tubing and matching misters are good sizes to use with the conversion.

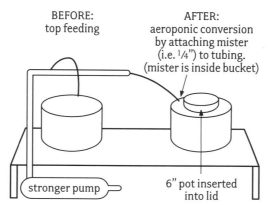

BEFORE:
top feeding

AFTER:
aeroponic conversion
by attaching mister
(i.e. ¼") to tubing.
(mister is inside bucket)

stronger pump

6" pot inserted
into lid

Basic changes from hydro to aero.

Option C: Top Feeding with PVC or Gutter Pipe
Tools
1. Drill and 3½-inch hole saw.
2. Knife.
3. Wrench.
4. Handsaw or skill saw.

Materials
1. One small mesh per plant (i.e. 3½ inches).
2. Two sawhorses to support the 8 to 12-foot lengths of pipe.
3. One alligator stake per plant.
4. One ⅛-inch fitting per plant.

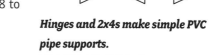

hinges

2x4

2x4s
connected
to hinges

2x4

legs

Hinges and 2x4s make simple PVC pipe supports.

5. One piece of ⅛-inch tubing connected from header line to an alligator stake per plant.
6. One reservoir.
7. Two 6-inch elbow fittings.

8. Six-inch pipe cut to equal lengths that are used to hold the plants.

9. Six-inch T-fittings for each length of 6-inch pipe, less the last pipe.

10. Mag drive pump.

11. Bypass valve.

12. ½-inch black poly tubing for header lines.

13. Two ½-inch black poly elbows.

14. ½-inch black poly Ts for each pipe, less the last pipe.

15. ½-inch black poly end cap for each that runs inside of the 6-inch pipe.

16. One 6 to 10-inch piece of PVC to connect drain line.

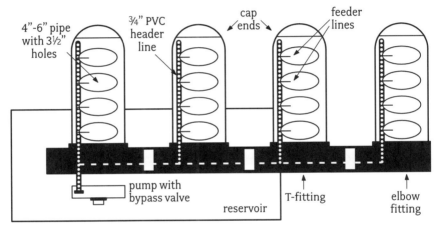

Top view of top-feeding pipe system.

Procedure

A. The 4 to 6-inch pipe will be placed on something that supports it. A quick sawhorse can be made with cheap 2x4-inch wood (i.e. 2 to 3-foot lengths) with hinges that the 2x4 wood slides into. Another 2x4 (i.e. an 8-foot length) is placed between the hinges to complete an instant sawhorse.

B. Two (or more) sawhorses can be used to support the connected pipes. Two sawhorses support an 8 to 12-foot length of 2x4-inch wood.

When the sawhorses are made, the side furthest from the reservoir should be the highest and at equal height. The side nearest the reservoir should be an inch or so lower for every 8-foot length so that the solution drains back into the reservoir.

C. All piping (i.e. 6-inch PVC) should be cut to the desired length.

D. Holes (3 ½ inches) should be cut in the pipe at the desired spacing (i.e. 8 to 12-inch centers). The hole sizes must match the pot sizes in order to make a custom fit.

E. All lengths of large pipe must have end caps attached to the higher ends (i.e 1-inch higher) that are located at the far side from the reservoir.

F. ½-inch poly tubing should be run along the inside of the pipes until it reaches the end. It should be cut to a length that reaches the middle of the T-fittings and elbow fitting that will be connected to the larger pipe at the shorter end. The ½-inch poly tubing must have a ½-inch end cap at the end. The ½-inch poly tubing should have small holes punched into the tubing at the desired spacing (i.e. 10-inch centers); it should have fittings (i.e. ³⁄₁₆, ⅛, ¼-inch) inserted into each of the holes; and it should haver a feeder line connected to the fitting.The appropriate sized tubing should be connected to the fittings in the header line. For example, ³⁄₁₆-inch tubing should be connected to a ³⁄₁₆-inch fitting. The tubing should be cut to a length that will reach the larger hole (for the pots) and with slack.

G. Small holes should be drilled into the pipe for the feeder tubing (i.e. ⅛, ³⁄₁₆, ¼-inch tubing) to be fed through. The hole should make for a snug fit.

H. All large 6-inch pipes (except the last pipe) are connected to their neighboring pipe with T-fittings. For example, 6-inch pipe will use 6-inch T-fittings. Small pieces of 6-inch pipe are placed between the T-fittings in order to connect the T-fittings and give the desired spacing (i.e. 10-inch centers).

I. The last pipe will have a 6-inch elbow fitting that connects to the 6-inch T-fitting of the second to last pipe. 6-inch pipe is placed between the 6-inch fittings.

J. The first 6-inch T-fitting (above the reservoir) can be connected to an elbow, then connected to larger pipe in order to send the solution downward into the reservoir without making a mess. A small piece of pipe is placed between the 6-inch T-fitting and elbow to secure the connection.

K. Another ½-inch poly line will run down through the 6-inch T-fittings and into the last elbow fitting of the large 6-inch pipe above the reservoir. This tubing will be connected to the other ½-inch poly tubing that runs through the lengths of pipe. All ½-inch tubing should have a ½-inch T-fitting inserted at the desired spacing (i.e. 10-inch centers), except for the very end. The very end will be attached to a ½-inch elbow. All of the fittings should be inserted before ½-inch tubing is run along the insides of the larger 6-inch T-fittings and elbow.

L. The ½-inch poly line with the ½-inch T-fittings and ½-inch elbow fitting should be run along the inside of the larger 6-inch T-fittings and elbow fittings.

M. The large 6-inch elbow fitting at the end (away from the reservoir) should be removed. The ½-inch elbow should be connected to the ½-inch line that runs through the inside of the large 6-inch pipe. Then the large 6-inch elbow and 6-inch T-fitting is reconnected. Piping and fittings can be glued with PVC cement (for PVC) pipe, but, the connections will be permanent. The system will not leak without glue; a little bit of duct tape can be used for securing connections so that disassembling is easy.

N. Each 6-inch T-fitting (starting from back to front) should be removed one at a time. When the 6-inch T-fitting is removed, the ½-inch poly lines should be connected together at the ½-inch T. Then, the larger pipe fittings are immediately connected back together after the smaller ½-inch tubing is connected to the inside of the larger T-fittings. Piping and fittings can be glued with PVC cement (for PVC) pipe, but, the connections will be permanent. The system will not leak without glue; a little bit of duct tape can be used for securing connections so that disassembling is easy.

O. At the first pipe (above the reservoir), there will be an open end of a ½-inch poly T. This loose end should be attached to a small piece (i.e. 3 inches) of ½-inch poly tubing. This tubing is connected to a ½-inch poly elbow. A proper length piece of ½-inch poly tubing is connected to the ½-inch elbow and connected to the pump. A ½-inch female fitting may need to be attached to the pump in order to connect the ½-inch tubing. This ½-inch tubing runs in the inside of the larger 6-inch piping.

P. Recommended Option: A ½-inch poly T should be inserted a few inches above the pump that sits at the bottom of the reservoir. A small piece (i.e. 3 Inches) of ½-inch poly tubing is connected to the ½-inch T. A bypass valve should be connected to the small piece of ½-inch tubing in order to control the flow rate.

Feeding
It is easiest to feed the plants with the pump timer running full-time, only during the light hours. A solar pump would run during these hours. But plants can be fed continuously (all day and all night). Also, plants can be fed intermittently (i.e. every 20 minutes for 2 minutes) during the light hours or perpertually.

Aeroponic Conversion
A. Each feeder line (i.e. ³⁄₁₆-inch) that is connected to a pot is removed.

B. A mister should be inserted to the end of the feeder line. Another small hole should be drilled for the mister to fit into. The holes in the pipe should be made in between the pots. The fit for the feeder line must be snug and secure. If the original line is too short, a new line must be cut and put in its place.

C. The pump should be changed to a high-pressure pump designed for aeroponics. The pump should be the size required for the garden dimensions.

Note: With this aeroponic conversion, plants will need to be top-fed until the roots go through the bottom of the medium. Then the plants can misted intermittently (i.e. every 20 minutes for 2 minutes) during light. hours, and one misting in the middle of darkness.

Option D: Column System #1
Top-feeding / Aeroponic System Using Pipe with Containers
Tools
1. Drill and 1-inch hole saw.
2. Exacto knife.
3. Crescent wrench.
4.A custom-sized hole saw (i.e. 3½-inch) for plant containers, if necessary.
5. Saw.

Materials

1. One mesh pot per plant (i.e. 2 inches), if necessary.
2. One ⅛ to ¼-inch fitting per plant.
3. One piece of ⅛-inch tubing per plant that is connected from header line to container.
4. One reservoir.
5. Six-inch pipe that is cut to equal lengths and that are used to hold the plants.
6. Pump.
7. Bypass valve.
8. ½-inch black poly tubing for header lines.
9. ½-inch black poly elbows.
10. ½-inch black poly Ts.
11. 1½-inch black poly end caps.
12. ¾-inch flex hose.
13. One bucket per pipe.
14. ¾-inch thru-hull fittings.
15. ¾-inch end cap.
16. 6ml black poly.
17. Twine.
18. Stones / gravel.

Plant-Holding Components

A. Choosing the desired pipe is the first step. Bigger pipe means there is more area for vegetation to cover. There are two options.

1. 4 to 8-inch PVC is a good pipe to use. Custom-sized holes should be cut into the pipe at the desired spacing (i.e. 8 to 12-inch centers). The hole sizes must match the size for the plant holders. The holders are special parts that may need to be tracked down. Some holders make space for a mesh pot while some holders are like a built-in mesh pot.

(A column systems that does not use plant containers is described a little further on in this book.)

2. This easiest option is to buy the pipe with the plant holders built into the plastic. They come with holders on one side for indoor systems, or holders on four sides for outdoor systems.

B. All piping (i.e. 4 to 8-inch PVC) should be cut to the desired height. For easy maintenance, the height should be less than the length of an outstretched arm so that a ladder is not needed while building the system.
Option: Pipe can be filled with medium.

C. All lengths of large pipe should have end caps (or 6ml plastic) attached to the top of the pipe in order to keep out the light.

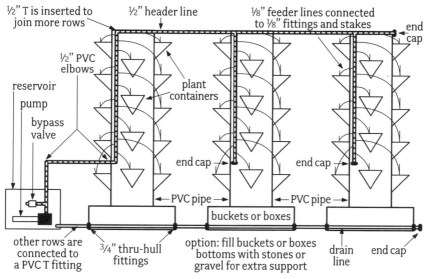

Column system for growing many small plants per square foot.

Drain Components

D. The buckets (or boxes) at the base of the piping should have holes made about 2 inches from the bottom on each side using a 1-inch hole saw for ¾-inch thru-hull fittings that will be inserted into each hole. Square plastic boxes, plastic buckets, or plywood boxes with two layers of black poly can be used. If plywood is used, care must be used when the thru-hull fittings are inserted because any rips will trap water under the plastic, which can lead to an overflow.

E. The pipes should be placed in the boxes with a snug fit. A hole saw or jigsaw is used to make the holes. Stones or gravel can be placed in the bucket or box in order to give extra support.

F. The reservoir should have a hole about 2 inches from the bottom that is made with a 1-inch hole saw. The hole should have a ¾-inch thru-hull fitting inserted into it. The end of the ¾-inch thru-hull fitting will be attached to the T-fitting from the drain line of the first bucket (or box).

G. The pipes should be placed in the desired locations.

H. Each row will have a T-fitting inserted at the end of the drain line that is nearest the reservoir. If ¾-inch flex hose is used, a ¾-inch PVC T will be used. If ½-inch poly hose is used, a ½-inch PVC T will be used to connect the rows together. ½-inch black poly is the cheapest option, but ¾-inch flex hose is the superior product. The last row will be have a 5-inch piece of tubing connected to the loose end of the PVC T, followed by an end cap. Using a PVC T is a good idea if more rows may be connected later.

Feeder Line Components

I.   1. A long piece of ½-inch poly tubing should be run along the tops of the pipes until it reaches the last one in the row. Twine and screw-in hooks can be used to keep it on top.
2. The front of the ½-inch poly tubing should have a ½-inch PVC elbow or PVC T inserted into it. A PVC T is used instead of the PVC elbow if more than one row is used.
3. The main line is then cut and a ½-inch PVC T is installed for each length of vertical pipe.
4. The PVC T is connected to pieces of ½-inch poly tubing that run down the sides of the large piping to a height just above the top of the reservoir.
5. The poly tubing is then connected to ½-inch PVC end caps.
6. The appropriate connection fittings that connect to the individual feeder lines should be inserted into the ½-inch header lines that run along the standing pipes. One fitting is used for each plant.
7. Lines are cut to a length that reaches each plant container with a little slack, and inserted into the connection fittings.
8. Lines are connected to alligator stakes.

J. The pump is connected to a piece of poly tubing that reaches the outside of the reservoir.

Option: A bypass valve can be inserted between the pump and the first ½-inch PVC elbow. To insert a bypass valve, a 1-inch chunk of the ½-inch poly line is cut out, a ½-inch PVC T is inserted, a 5-inch chunk of ½-inch poly plastic is connected, and a lightweight plastic tap is attached to the 5-inch chunk of black poly.

K. The end of the line is connected to a ½-inch PVC elbow.

L. The ½-inch PVC elbow is connected to a piece of ½-inch poly tubing that reaches the tubing that hangs down from the front of the first pipe.

M. A ½-inch PVC elbow is used to connect these last two loose ends.

Feeding

It is easiest to feed the plants with the pump timer running full-time only during the light hours. A solar pump runs during light hours. But plants can be fed continuously (all day and all night). Also, plants can be fed intermittently (i.e. every 20 minutes for 2 minutes, or every 2 to 5 minutes for 15 to 30 seconds).

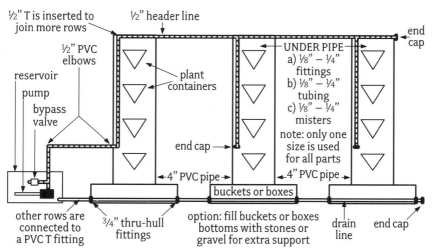

Single slot column system made from 1 to 8-inch pipe.

Aeroponic Conversion

Making the aeroponic version of this system is easier than making the top-feeding system.

A. The lines that run down the outsides of the column will now run inside. The appropriate misters should be inserted into the ends of the smallest tubing (i.e. ⅛-inch).

B. The pump should be changed to a high-pressure pump designed for aeroponics. The pump should be the size required for the garden dimensions.

Option E: Column System #2
Top-Feeding Using Plastic Sacks
Tools
1. Exacto knife.
2. Crescent wrench.

Materials
1. One reservoir for feeding.
2. One reservoir for flushing.
3. Plastic horticulture sacks
4. Pump.
5. Bypass valve.
6. ½-inch black poly tubing for header lines, ⅛-inch poly for feeder lines.
7. ½-inch black poly elbows.
8. ½-inch black poly Ts.
9. ½-inch black poly end caps.
10. ¾-inch flex hose.
11. One bucket per pipe to collect runoff solution.
12. ¾-inch thru-hull fittings.
13. ¾-inch end cap.
14. Twine.

Plant-Holding Components
A. Plastic horticulture sacks are filled up with medium (i.e. soilless mix). Bigger sacks give more area for vegetation to cover.

B. All sacks should be hung from a sturdy beam. For easy maintenance, the height should be less than the length of an outstretched arm so that a grower does not need to use a ladder while building the system.

The sacks should be placed in the desired locations, such as rows.

C. Small drain holes should be inserted into the bottoms of the sacks.

Drain Components

D. The buckets (or boxes) at the base of the sacks should have holes made about 2 inches from the bottom on each side using a 1-inch hole saw. ¾-inch thru-hull fittings are then inserted into each hole. Square plastic boxes, plastic buckets, or plywood boxes with two layers of black poly can be used. If plywood is used, care must be used when the thru-hull fittings are inserted because any rips will trap water under the plastic, which can lead to the solution overflowing.

E. The sacks should drain into the buckets without making a mess.

F. The reservoir should have a hole about 2 inches from the bottom that is made with a 1-inch hole saw. A ¾-inch thru-hull fitting is inserted into the hole; the end of the ¾-inch thru-hull fitting will be attached to the T-fitting from the drain line of the first bucket (or box) with ½-inch poly tubing (or ¾-inch flex hose).

G. Each row will have a T-fitting inserted at the end of the drain line that is nearest the reservoir. If ¾-inch flex hose is used, a ¾-inch PVC T will be used. For ½-inch tubing, ½-inch or ¾-inch fittings can be used for all drain parts. ½-inch black poly is the cheapest option, but ¾-inch flex hose is the superior product. The last row will be have a 5-inch piece of tubing connected to the loose end of the PVC T, followed by an end cap. Using a PVC T is a good idea if more rows may be connected later.

H. The sacks are soaked until the medium is saturated. Then, they can be refilled and remoistened if necessary.

I. Holes are cut in the sacks for the plants with the exacto knife. It is recommended that you know what area a plant will cover until harvest so that the holes can be made in precise locations. It may take a crop or two to figure this one out.

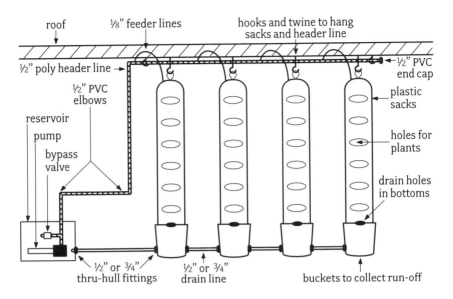

Plastic sacks ready to support a vertical garden.

Feeder Line Components

J. 1. A long piece of ½-inch poly tubing should be run along the support beam so that it reaches near all of the sack tops. Twine and screw-in hooks can be used to keep it in position. An end cap should be inserted at the end.

2. The front of the ½-inch poly tubing should have a ½-inch PVC elbow or PVC T inserted into it. A PVC T is used instead of the PVC elbow if more than one row is used.

3. The small ⅛-inch poly tubing is then connected to the ½-inch main line with the appropriate connection fittings that connect to the individual feeder lines. A hole punch is used to make the hole for the connectors.

4. Lines are cut to a length that reaches the top of each sack. Only one line per sack is used.

5. Lines are then connected to alligator stakes.

K. The pump is connected to a piece of poly tubing that reaches the outside of the reservoir.

Option: A bypass valve can be inserted between the pump and the first ½-inch PVC elbow. To insert a bypass valve, a 1-inch chunk is cut out of the ½-inch poly line, a $\frac{1}{2}$-inch PVC T is inserted, a 5-inch chunk of $\frac{1}{2}$-inch poly plastic is connected to the PVC T, and a lightweight plastic tap is attached to the 5-inch chunk of 5-inch black poly.

L. The end of the line from the pump is connected to a $\frac{1}{2}$-inch PVC elbow.

M. The $\frac{1}{2}$-inch PVC elbow is connected to a piece of $\frac{1}{2}$-inch poly tubing that reaches the tubing that hangs down from the front of the first sack.

N. A $\frac{1}{2}$-inch PVC elbow is used to connect the lines that run along the roof beam to the tubing running from the pump.

Feeding

Plants can be fed continually or intermittently with the pump running on a timer. Continually can be full-time, or only during light hours. A solar pump would run in the light hours without a timer.

Intermittently means a timer can run the pump every 20 minutes (for a few minutes), or every 2 days for a few hours or so. Plants will grow fine as long as the medium does not dry up. Feeding every few days is the easiest way, but growth will be slower than plants fed with continual feeding.

Drain to Waste Conversion

The entire drain system mentioned in steps 4 to 7 can be eliminated. If this is the case, it is recommended that you feed so that everything stays saturated, yet the runoff through the drain holes in the plastic sacks is minimal.

NFT (Nutrient Film Technique)

With nutrient film technique, plants can be fed with continuous or intermittent film that is pumped through a header line, then drained down a trough, PVC pipe, or flood table. The solution travels down the bottom of the trough where it collects in the reservoir, before it is recirculated. The solution can run all day.

Capillary matting can be placed under trough.

Air pumps can be used to aerate the nutrient solution.

Automatic thermostatic heat cords can be placed around a reservoir to keep the solution warm. Chillers cool the reservoir.

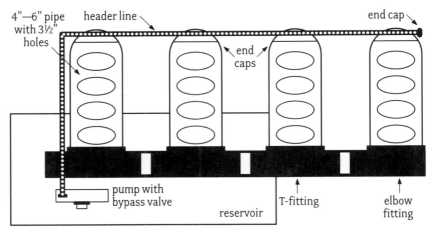

Schematic diagram of an NFT system supported on cement blocks.

The only difference in building this system from the top-feeding system on pages 29 to 33 is the header line. The ½-inch poly or PVC header line runs along the side, then it connects to a matching elbow. Then it runs along the back of the pipes until it reaches the end. The header line is end-capped at the end. Only one feeder line is connected to the header line on each each pipe to deliver the solution down the pipe.

Aeroponics

Aeroponics is basically hydroponics, but with a twist. Instead of using a growing medium to anchor roots and to run a solution through, the roots are suspended in air and are fed with periodic mistings (set on a timer).

A simple aeroponic system can be built by placing 2-inch styrofoam on top of a solid, leak-free table. It is best to have the root environment well draining so that roots don't sit in a few inches of slow-moving water.

Another alternative is using PVC pipe or gutter pipe to hold plants in place and to allow the solution to drain back into the reservoir.

One more method is to use a small mesh pot inserted into a larger pail (i.e. 5 to 7 gallons).

Aeroponics can also be of assistance to novice growers for the fact that there is less medium (e.g. clay) to hold salts that hinder growth. However there are hydroponic methods that use mediums that do not absorb many salts (e.g. perlite).

A disadvantage of an aeroponic system is the higher cost of a high-powered pump that is necessary to create a highly aerated mist. Another disadvantage is when large gardens have clogged misters from specialty plant foods, such as humic acid. When misters get clogged during hot hours, there is only so much time to fix the problem before the wilting damage is irreparable.

Homemade Aeroponics
Tools
1. Drill and 1½ to 2-inch hole saw.
2. Knife.
3. Wrench.
4. Handsaw or skill saw.

Materials
1. One small mesh pot per plant (i.e. 2 inches).
2.Two sawhorses to support the 8 to 12 lengths of pipe.
3. One mister per plant.
4. One ⅛ to ¼-inch fitting per plant.
5.One piece of ⅛ to ¼-inch tubing connected from header line to mister per plant.
6. One reservoir.
7. Two 6-inch elbow fittings.
8. Six-inch pipe cut to equal lengths that are used to hold the plants.
9. Six-inch T-fittings for each length of 6-inch pipe, less the last pipe.
10. High-powered pump.
11. Bypass valve.
12. ½-inch black poly tubing for header lines.
13. Two ½-inch black poly elbows.
14. ½-inch black poly Ts for each pipe, less the last pipe.
15. ½-inch black poly end cap for each that runs inside of the 6-inch pipe.
16. One 6 to 10-inch length of 6-inch pipe to connect the drain lines.

Procedure
A. The 4 to 6-inch pipe will be placed on something that supports it. A quick sawhorse can be made with cheap 2x4-inch wood (i.e. 2 to 3-foot lengths) with hinges that the 2x4-inch wood slides into. Another 2x4 (i.e. an 8-foot length) is placed between the hinges to complete an instant sawhorse.

B. Two (or more) sawhorses can be used to support the connected pipes. Two sawhorses support an 8 to 12 length of 2x4-inch wood.

When the sawhorses are made, the side furthest from the reservoir should be the highest and at equal height.

The side nearest the reservoir should be an inch or so lower for every 8-foot length so that the solution drains back into the reservoir.

C. All piping (i.e. 6-inch PVC) should be cut to the desired length.

D. Holes (i.e. 1½-inch) should be cut in the pipe at the desired spacing (i.e. 8 to 12-inch centers). The hole sizes must match the pot sizes in order to make a custom fit.

E. All lengths of large pipe must have end caps attached to the higher ends that are located at the far end away from the reservoir.

F. ½-inch poly tubing should be run along the inside of the pipes until it reaches the end. It should be cut to a length that reaches the middle of the T-fittings and elbow fittings that will be connected to the larger pipe at the shorter end. The ½-inch poly tubing must have a ½-inch end cap at the end. The ½-inch poly tubing should have small holes punched into the tubing at the desired spacing (i.e. 10-inch centers), it should have fittings (i.e. ⅛, ³⁄₁₆, ¼-inch) inserted into each of the holes, and it should have a line (approximately 1-inch) inserted into the fitting before it is strung through the 6-inch pipe. The appropriate sized tubing should be connected to the fittings in the header line. For example, ³⁄₁₆-inch tubing should be connected to a ³⁄₁₆-inch fitting. The tubing should be cut to a length that will reach in between the larger holes (for the pots) with a little slack.

G. Small holes should be drilled into the pipe for the feeder tubing (i.e. ⅛, ³⁄₁₆, ¼-inch tubing) to be fed through. The hole should be a tight fit.

H. A mister should be inserted into the end of the feeder line. Another small hole should be drilled for the mister to fit into. The holes in the pipe should be made in between the pots. The fit with the mister must be snug and secure.

I. All large pipes (except the last pipe) are connected to their neighboring pipe with T-fittings. For example, 6-inch pipe will use 6-inch T-fittings. Small pieces of pipe are placed between the T-fittings in order to connect the T-fittings and give the desired spacing (i.e. 10-inch centers).

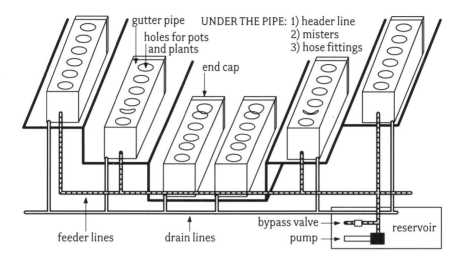

This aeroponic garden has a v-shape.

J. The last 6-inch pipe will have an elbow fitting that connects to the T-fitting of the second-to-last pipe.

K. The first 6-inch T-fitting can be connected to an elbow, then connected to larger pipe in order to send the solution downward into the reservoir without making a mess. A small piece of pipe is placed between the T-itting and elbow fitting to secure the connection.

L. Another ½-inch poly line will run down through the 6-inch T-fittings and into the last 6-inch elbow fitting of the large pipe above the reservoir. This tubing will be connected to the other ½-inch poly tubing that runs through the lengths of 6-inch pipe. All ½-inch tubing should have a ½-inch T-fitting inserted at the desired spacing (i.e. 10-inch centers), except for the very end. The very end wilbe attached to a ½-inch elbow. All of the fittings should be inserted before ½-inch tubing is run along the insides of the larger T-fittings and elbow.

M. The ½-inch poly line with the ½-inch T-fittings and elbow fitting should be run along the inside of the larger T-fittings and elbow fitting.

N. The large elbow fitting at the end (away from the reservoir) should be removed. The ½-inch elbow should be connected to the ½-inch line that runs through the inside of the large pipe. Then the large 6-inch elbow and 6-inch T-fitting is reconnected. Piping and fittings can be glued with PVC cement (for PVC) pipe, but, the connections will be permanent. The system will not leak without glue; a little bit of duct tape can be used for securing connections so that disassembling is easy.

O. Each 6-inch T-fitting (starting from back to front) should be removed one at a time. When the 6-inch T-fitting is removed, the ½-inch poly lines should be connected together at the ½-inch T. Then the larger pipe fittings are immediately connected back together after the smaller ½-inch tubing is connected to the inside of the larger 6-inch T-fittings. Piping and fittings can be glued with PVC cement (for PVC) pipe, but, the connections will be permanent. The system will not leak without glue; a little bit of duct tape can be used for securing connections so that disassembling is easy.

P. At the first 6-inch pipe (above the reservoir), there will be an open end of a ½-inch poly T. This loose end should be attached to a small piece (say, 3 inches) of ½-inch poly tubing. This tubing is connected to a ½-inch poly elbow. A proper length piece of ½-inch poly tubing is connected to the ½-inch elbow and connected to the pump. A ½-inch female fitting may need to be attached to the pump in order to connect the ½-inch tubing. This ½-inch tubing runs in the inside of the larger piping.

Q. Recommended Option: A ½-inch poly T should be inserted a few inches above the pump that sits at the bottom of the reservoir. A small piece (say, 3 inches) of ½-inch poly tubing is connected to the ½-inch T. A bypass valve should be connected to the small piece of ½-inch tubing in order to control the flow rate.

R. The high-pressure pump should be the size required for the garden dimensions.

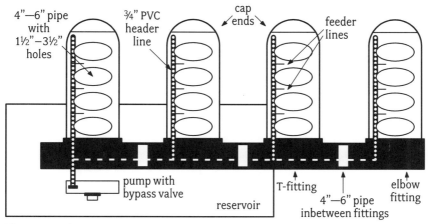

Flat aeroponic system.

More Aeroponic Systems

Most hydroponic feeding systems can be converted to aeroponic systems with:

1. A high-pressure pump.
2. Misters / feeder lines to mist the roots.
3. Leak-proofing if necessary.

In the top-feeding section, there are examples of systems that can easily be converted to aeroponic systems.

Feeding

It is easiest to feed the plants with the pump timer running full-time, only during the light hours. But plants can be fed continuously (all day and all night). Also, plants can be fed intermittently (i.e. every 20 minutes for 2 minutes) during the light hours, and once in the night.

Soilless Mix Systems

Soilless mix composed chiefly of peat moss is unquestionably the most versatile horticultural medium. It comes under trade names such as Sunshine Mix™ and Jiffy Mix™.

If plenty is used, feeding could be as minimal as once a week when the medium begins to dry out. Soilless mix is best used to keep the workload down because it retains a lot of moisture and nutrients between periodic feedings.

Feeding immediately after it is daylight or when lights start up is a good time to periodically saturate this medium.

Nevertheless, if soilless mix is fed continuously with a top-feeding hydroponic system, plant growth will be much faster. Note that flow rate is critical with Sunshine Mix™. If the flow is too fast, water will form puddles and overflow out of the containers. With soilless mix, continuous feeding works best with slow feeding and large containers.

Another way to run solution through soilless mix is to set an intermittent timer to operate for a couple of minutes at a time, several times per day (i.e. 6 times).

Soilless mix systems are discussed on pages 48 to 75. Soilless Mix Improvisation on pages 56 to 75 gives popular methods for low-maintenance outdoor gardens.

Billy Bob's Organic Hydroponic System, Using Soilless Mix
Complete Set-Up
Materials
1. Two plastic flood tables, available at hydroponic shops; or two sheets of ¾-inch plywood, six pieces of 1x2-inch wood (cheapest), and 17 feet of 10-foot wide black poly plastic (thick). Available at hardware stores or building supply shops. Custom sizing may be needed for a particular room size. As an easier option, plant dishes, which are cheap and available at garden centers, can be placed under the containers.
2. Sawhorses to support tables.
3. One 5-gallon bucket for each flood table, to catch runoff solution. Found all over the place.
4. One or two bales (3.0 to 8 cubic feet) of Sunshine® #2 mix, unfertilized Pro-Mix™, Jiffy Mix™, or other unfertilized soilless mix that is pH buffered at near neutral (6.0 to 7.0) and is mainly composed of peat, perlite, and lime. Available at garden centers, mercantile wholesalers, and hydroponic shops. Bales are often found in 2.0- and 3.8-cubic feet sizes. (Room size is the important factor in determining the correct size.) Note: one bale fills about ten 5-gallon containers.
5. 2 to 20 buckets (or 2 to 20 nursery pots). The number of buckets depends on the size of the room. Smaller gallon buckets (1 to 3-gallon sizes) are good for growing a large number of small plants. Larger containers (5 to 20-gallon buckets) are

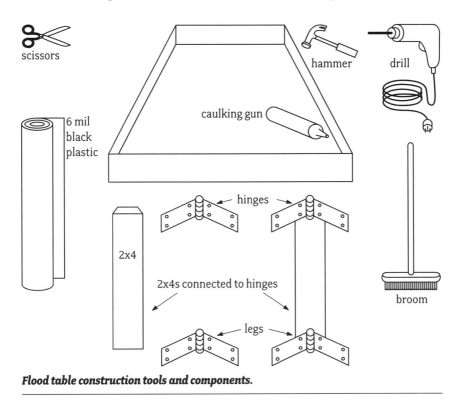

Flood table construction tools and components.

good for growing a small number of large plants. Both methods are effective.
6. Fertilizing materials. (Feeding and formulas are discussed on pages 84 to 103.)

Procedure

A. Now that the basic set-up is out of the way, the mix comes next. A tarp should be laid down for placing and breaking up the chunks of soilless mix.

B. Several drainage holes (up to 75% hole space, meaning that only 25% of the bottom will be showing plastic) should be inserted into the bucket bottoms, using a sharp knife, unless nursery containers with premade holes are used.

C. The containers with the mix can be placed on a flood table. Directions for building a flood table are described on pages 19 to 21. A simpler alternative to the flood table is to use plant dishes to catch runoff solution, or a bucket placed under each flood table to catch the runoff solution.

A respirator or at least some sort of dust mask should be worn when mixing all of the components. If care is not taken here, materials such as soilless mix and other fertilizers can get into the lungs.

The buckets should be filled about one-inch from the top with the soilless mixture.

The buckets are watered until they get a good soaking.

D. Plants can now be transplanted into the mix.

Other Mix-Making Options

An option is to add earthworm castings (9kg (20lbs) of castings per 3.8 to 4.0 cubic feet bale) and / or ¼ to ½ bag of perlite or vermiculite. Adding inexpensive perlite is recommended for extra aeration in the mix and for its pH near neutral (7.0) characteristic.

The mix in this program is actually of organic hydroponic quality; to qualify in the soilless mix category, a formula must be less than 10% inorganic soil. This formula is much more than 90% soilless. The organic peat, gypsum, dolomite lime, earthworm castings, and perlite all qualify as soilless.

Technical Add-ons
Option A: Flood and Drain Add-on

Instead of feeding the plants periodically from the top, the plants can be fed from flooding and draining the bottom roots.

The plants will adjust and roots will feed while growing out the bottoms of the containers. This will be more productive than regular feeding. Plants will no longer need to be fed from the top.

When the top of the mix stays wet, air to the roots is lost. However, if the top of the mix stays wet, this moisture will act like a parachute if anything goes wrong with flooding and draining, such as perlite compaction clogging a filter, or bat guano clogging up panty hose which will restrict the pumping capacity of the pump.

Adding this flood and drain option is possible during any part of the program. (Building a flood and drain system is discussed in this chapter on pages 19 to 21.)

Watering made easy.

Option B: Top-Feeding Add-on

Plants can be fed periodically or continuously with top feeding. For organic fertilizers, ¼-inch lines are recommended. Plants can be top-fed in the soilless mix, or they can be transplanted into a larger container of a different grow medium, such as clay, and then top-fed from there. (Top-feeding details and full set-up are explained in this chapter on pages 29 to 33.)

Option C: Drip-Watering System

Hand-watering can be done relatively quickly and is, of course, the cheapest way to go. However, installing a drip system (with or without a computer timer) may allow for easy living. With a drip system, gravity causes liquid to flow from a high elevation downward into the pots.

Note: The materials for this drip system use ¼-inch sizes for the lines, barbed fittings and drippers. But, ⅛-inch sizes can be used for the lines, barbed fittings and drippers can be used as a replacement.

Tools

1. Drill.
2. One-inch hole saw.
3. A small drill bit (less than ⅛-inch).
4. Handsaw.

Materials

1. A container that holds at least 2 quarts (liters) per plant.
2. ¾-inch thru-hull fitting with O-ring.
3. Tap (for turning off and on).
4. PVC fitting with a ¾-inch threaded female end and a ½-inch end for the polybutylene tubing to fit on.
5. ½-inch PVC end cap.
6. ⅛-inch barbed fittings to plug into header line (one for each plant).
7. ¼-inch drippers; one per plant.
8. 20 feet of ½-inch polybutylene tubing (or what is needed).
9. 50 feet and probably more of ⅛-inch polybutylene tubing.
10. Silicone.
11. In-line filter unit and filter with ¾-inch threads (male and female).
12. Computerized water timer (optional) Should be available at garden centers, hydroponic shops, and water supply businesses.
13. Support system for the reservoir.
14. Sandpaper for plastic (any coarseness).
15. One small c-clamp (optional).
16. Hole punch for ⅛-inch fittings into header line.
17. Teflon tape.

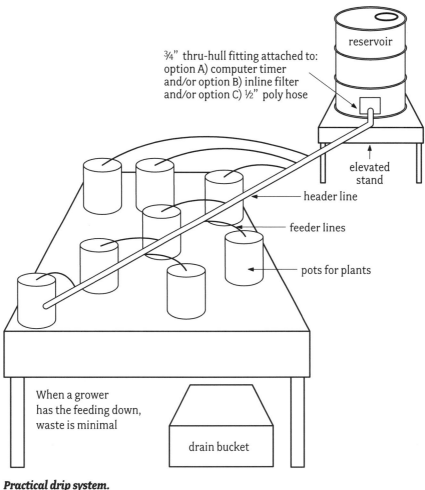

¾" thru-hull fitting attached to:
option A) computer timer
and/or option B) inline filter
and/or option C) ½" poly hose

reservoir

elevated
stand

header line

feeder lines

pots for plants

When a grower
has the feeding down,
waste is minimal

drain bucket

Practical drip system.

Procedure

A. Using a 1-inch hole saw, a 1-inch hole is drilled into the side of the reservoir, 2 to 3 inches from the bottom.

B. Inserting the ¾-inch thru-hull fitting into the 1-inch hole is next. The O-ring is on the inside of the reservoir, and the threads are on the outside of the can.

C. The fitting should be cut at the end of the threads located furthest from the garbage can. This cut should be vertical and uniform. The plastic particulate

Holding tank connected to hose.

must be sanded before screwing the tap on. Teflon tape can be placed on the threads in order to prevent leaks.

D. The in-line filter is connected. This will give decent results and be easy to clean. The entire water-holding unit should be located high in the corner of the room. A platform built of plywood scraps (or other junk) gives support for the liquid solutions.

E. Optional. The computerized timer can be fastened. If it is not included, then the female end of the ¾-inch PVC fitting is fastened to the in-line filter.

F. The ½-inch tubing should be gently connected to the last fitting so that it is secure, yet allows for easy removal of the line to clean the filter. This should hold sufficiently, but a small c-clamp may also be added to the connection for extra safety.

G. ½-inch tubing is extended diagonally across the garden until it reaches the far end corner of a flood table and rests on the surface.

H. The end of the ½-inch tubing is cut, and the ½-inch end cap is inserted. That joint may be c-clamped.

I. Somewhere along the lower elevated part of the header line (but higher than the containers), holes should be punched into the line. The number of holes should be equal to the number of plant containers.

J. Small holes are drilled into the tops of the containers (above the mix) for the ⅛-inch tubing to be inserted snugly, or the tubing can be placed into alligator stakes. If too many holes are made by accident, plugs can be used to fill the holes.

K. The ½-inch tubing is linked between each individual ⅛-inch fitting from the header and each individual plant, without leaving too much slack.

L. If there are any leaks in the polybutylene after testing (such as leaks in the joints), silicone can be used to seal leaks. Silicone must be applied to dry tubing and it must be allowed to dry.

M. As plants get larger and need to be spaced out, more ⅛-inch tubing will be needed to replace some of the existing tubing. Tubing can be reused.

N. Optional
Drippers can be inserted into the end of each line to control the flow rate. They can be purchased in rates like 2½ quarts (or litres) per hour. Drippers allow the

water to stay in an area about one-foot in diameter.

This drip system will be trouble-free when plain water is passed through the tubing.

Some fertilizers, such as bat guano and Sea mix™, water with particulate, and other forms of debris can clog the in-line filter, the ⅛-inch fittings, or the ½-inch tubing. However, many fertilizing mixes will not clog the lines. Monitor the system carefully so that disasters such as plants going without solution do not occur. Cleaning the filter frequently by rinsing it with plain water and removing the ½-inch end cap and flushing the system with plain water is a useful maintenance.

Blowing or sucking the ends of ⅛-inch end tubing helps remove clogs. But if that is necessary, a flush of the system may be necessary.

If the computer timer is part of the setup, it should be set to run for plenty of time, so that it will not shut off during the drip process. Using the computer is risky business, because it may be used when nobody is at the site. Why else would it be needed? If the site is vacated, electronic malfunctions, battery failure, clogs in the system, or fluke leaks are all possible. Leaks should not occur in any system that uses tubing to deliver solution to the plants. But, should one occur, silicone applied to clean, dry plastic will seal a leak.

Going without the computer and taking advantage of the ease of a drip system is already beneficial.

Soilless Mix Improvisation
Soilless Mix / Forest Compost / Peat Moss
Step 1: Planning the Garden Dimensions or
Determining the Container Size.
Matching the right plant to the right place is the secret to success.

Option A: The Underground Garden
Digging a hole 1 to 2 feet deep in spring or up to a month before transplanting gives a plant a place to grow in the ground. The hole's diameter should fall between 1 to 4 feet, though 1 to 2-foot holes may be preferred for smaller plants or non-bumper-crop years. The four-footer used in a hot summer in full sun would be a high-yielding, low-maintenance choice.

Another option is to dig a 1 to 2-foot deep trench that is 1-foot wide (or more).

Budding plant in grow bag.

Where should the digging take place?

In *sandy soil* if it is possible to water frequently in hot summer months. Excellent for regular feedings, sand helps warm the soil.

In *clay soil* if decent water and nutrient retention is wanted so that only a few visits are needed. Clay soil is cooler than sandy soil.

In *bog soil* if it is not too mucky. Good bog soil / peat will compact when it is squeezed and crumble when it is broken up. Watering is eliminated in a good bog. A grower must be careful because a good bog one year may flood in another year. Developing a relationship with the water table is necessary when planting in a bog. If the bog contains water pools and it is coated with sphagnum peat moss, flooding should not be a problem, even in the wettest years.

On a *rock cliff.* Here, instead of a digging a hole, the site is made 2 to 4 feet high with mix. This is the best bet for a wet season because of drainage, electromagnetism possibilities, and the possibilities of altering root temperature for proper warmth.

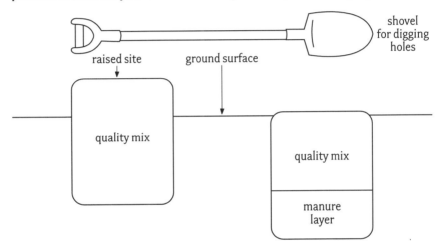

Left: Raised site for warmer roots. Right: Typical hole for mix.

Option B: Container Garden

Using the proper container size is the first step. In other words, how big should the plants be grown? All things being equal in the mix, the larger the container, the larger the plant. However, to grow the larger plants, capitalizing on a full growing season is a must. Late-starting plants have a limited growth potential, so in this case growers often use more plants to grow big buds on the smaller plants.

For the highest possible yield when putting plants out in the early spring after the last threat of frost, it is recommended to use at least 15 to 20 gallons of mix per plant in a garbage bag, garbage can, or a box 3 feet square x 2 feet

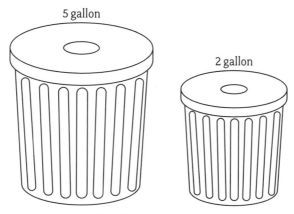

Common container sizes for small and larger plants.

high (all well-draining). For smaller plants and late starts, using less mix is less wasteful.

A 1 to 3-inch layer of mushroom manure or steer manure in the bottom of the containers will provide nutritional fuel for the feeder roots that will bunch up at the bottom. Forgetting to feed the bottom roots is probably the biggest omission in the plant's diet, unless supplemental feedings are frequently applied. A layer on the bottom cuts down on feeding maintenance.

For late transplanting, using a container ranging from 2 to 5 gallons will work fine, depending on how much of the season will be dedicated to vegetative growth. For example, in Northwest Washington State, a female clone transplanted in July may begin to flower soon after the transplant, leaving only a top flower. Therefore, a 2-gallon container will be sufficient. Lining up all the containers side by side and growing a Sea of Green is a possibility when small plants are grown for the top buds. Another female clone may vegetate for 2 months, and finish flowering in mid-October. In this case, a 3 to 5-gallon container could fill up with roots.

Getting to know strains inside and out allows a grower to learn how to match the right plant with the right container.

The advantage of container plants is that they can be brought indoors to finish budding (i.e. at 2 to 3 weeks) under lights. This can make some plants more potent, looking like they were grown indoors. Some plants will be less potent grown outdoors. Sometimes when plants are grown outdoors, making a quick decision is part of the program, such as saving plants from molding.

Step 2: Making a Top-Quality Mix for the Plants

A quality homemade mix can be made with peat moss or forest compost, or may be prepared with a soilless mix that is purchased from the store. Store-bought goods are easier to work with because the pH is at the desired level and it is mixed with perlite and / or vermiculite, lime, and other goodies. On the other hand, homemade mixes are a lot cheaper, often less than half the price.

When soilless mix is purchased, it is sterilized and has a pH that needs no further adjusting. However, forest compost and peat moss can be substituted with soilless mix. The key is to get the pH right (5.5 to 7.0). Most forest compost has a pH of 5.2 to 5.5, while peat moss has a pH of 4.0 to 5.5, depending upon the source. When perlite and lime are added to peat moss or forest compost, the outcome is a basic soilless mix.

Here is a formula to raise the pH and prepare a quality mix using forest compost or peat moss:

A. A 20-gallon garbage can (like the cheap Rubbermaid®) is filled ⅔ full with rich, black forest compost or peat moss.

B. Perlite is then added to the top. Then the mix is mixed thoroughly in the can, or it can be emptied onto the ground and mixed with a pitchfork or gloves. A respirator or good dust mask should be worn for all mixing.

C. 5 to 6 cups of fine dolomite lime and ¾ to 1 cup of hydrated lime is added and thoroughly mixed in.

Forest compost and peat moss are good mediums for affordable homemade recipes. A grower can make homemade mixes before following the examples for adding fertilizers to the homemade soilless mix. The pH should be higher than 5.5 and less than 7.0.

Forest compost comes from a mature forest. It exists in a mature forest under a layer of sticks and needles. It is located a few inches beneath the needle layer. Some stores sell forest compost mixtures. It is usually free of stones and has a pH greater than 5. All loose roots should be removed from forest compost before it is used.

Peat moss comes from peat bogs. Peat bogs exist in areas of poor drainage that stay wet all year long.

D. A fertilizer combination is added to the soilless mix. There are 8 recipe examples on the next pages.

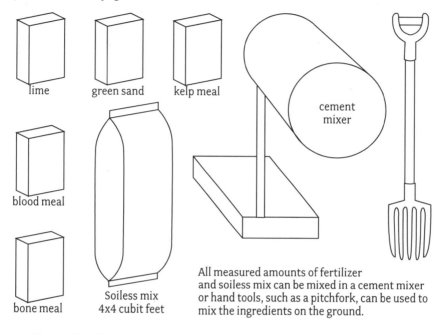

lime

green sand

kelp meal

cement mixer

blood meal

bone meal

Soiless mix
4x4 cubit feet

All measured amounts of fertilizer and soiless mix can be mixed in a cement mixer or hand tools, such as a pitchfork, can be used to mix the ingredients on the ground.

Fertilizer and soilless mix are ready to blend.

Organic Fertilizing Recipes for Soilless Mix, Forest Compost, and Peat Moss Mix

Note: mix without soil is classed as organic hydroponic.

1. Four 3.8 to 4 cubic foot bales of Sunshine® #2 Mix, Jiffy Mix™, Pro Mix™, or other soilless mix.
2. Four bags of composted steer manure (20 to 30 quarts each bag).
3. One gallon of blood meal.
4. One gallon of steamed bonemeal.
5. One gallon of greensand.
6. Two quarts of kelp meal.
7. 0 to 50 quarts of perlite and / or 0 to 50 quarts of vermiculite.
8. Up to one-third parts soil.

1. One 3.8 to 4.0 cubic foot bale of Sunshine® #2 Mix, Jiffy Mix™, Pro Mix™, or other soilless mix.
2. One 10kg bag of Welcome Harvest Farm™ Flower Power.
3. ½ to 1 bag of composted steer manure (10 to 30 quarts).
4. One quart of alfalfa meal.
5. 0 to 40 quarts of perlite.
6. Up to one-third parts soil.

1. One 3.8 to 4.0 cubic foot bale of Sunshine® #2 Mix, Jiffy Mix™, or Pro Mix™.
2. 5kg of Welcome Harvest Farm™ Flower Power.
3. One 20 to 30 quart bag of composted steer manure.
4. Eight cups of canola meal.
5. Three cups of blood meal.
6. 1 quart of greensand.
7. Perlite and vermiculite, as desired.
8. Up to one-third parts soil.

1. One 3.8 to 4.0 cubic foot bale of Sunshine #2 Mix™, Jiffy Mix™, or Pro Mix™.
2. ½ bag (10 to 15 quarts) of chicken manure.
3. ½ bag (10 to 15 quarts) of composted steer manure.
4. Four cups of blood meal.
5. Four cups of kelp meal.
6. Four cups of greensand.
7. Four cups of steamed bonemeal (pellet form).
8. 0 to 4 quarts (liters) well-decomposed compost.
9. 0 to 50 quarts of any combination of perlite and vermiculite.
10. Up to one-third parts soil.

1. One 3.8 to 4.0 cubic foot bale of Sunshine® #2 Mix, Jiffy Mix™, Pro Mix™, or other soilless mix.
2. One bag of mushroom manure (20 to 30 quarts [liters]).
3. Two cups of langbeinite.
4. Four cups of greensand.
5. Four cups of kelp meal.
6. One quart of blood meal.

7. One quart of steamed bonemeal.
8. 2.2kg of Welcome Harvest Farm™ Flower Power.
9. 0 to 30 quarts of vermiculite and / or perlite.
10. Up to one-third parts soil.

1. One 3.8 to 4.0 cubic foot bale of Sunshine® #2 Mix, Jiffy Mix™, Pro Mix™, or other soilless mix.
2. 9kg (20lbs) of pure earthworm castings (beware of imitators).
3. One 20 to 30 quart bag of composted steer manure.
4. One 5kg bag of Welcome Harvest Farm™ Flower Power.
5. Perlite / vermiculite combination, as desired.
6. Up to one-third parts soil.

1. One 3.8 to 4.0 cubic foot bale of Sunshine® #2 Mix, Jiffy Mix™, Pro Mix™, or other soilless mix.
2. 9kg (20lbs) of pure earthworm castings.
3. One 20 to 30 quart bag of composted steer manure.
4. One quart of blood meal.
5. Two quarts of steamed bonemeal.
6. One quart of kelp meal.
7. One quart of greensand.
8. 0 to 50 quarts or any perlite / vermiculite combination.
9. Up to one-third parts soil.

1. One 3.8 to 4.0 cubic foot bale of Sunshine® #2 Mix, Jiffy Mix™, Pro Mix™, or other soilless mix.
2. 9kg (20lbs) of pure earthworm castings.
3. 20 quarts of well decomposed compost.
4. One quart of bonemeal.
5. One quart of greensand.
6. 0 to 50 quarts of any perlite / vermiculite combination.
7. Up to one-third parts soil.

Why is soilless mix used?
It is made from organic peat, which holds nutrients, moisture, and air very

effectively. It is versatile for all climates, and the grower has complete control over the fertilizing of the grow medium. Also, it is pH buffered which allows pH control. To put it simply, it allows the grower to get high-end results with minimal effort, for it does most of the work.

Calcium peroxide, available under many trade names, can be added to any mixture. It breaks down into oxygen and lime.

Other Organic Fertilizer Substitutes
Nitrogen
Some people don't like using blood meal, although it is one of the cheapest and strongest-acting dried nitrogen sources for the amount used. The numbers on the organic fertilizer packs do not represent the nitrogen of value to the plant, they represent the percentage of the fertilizer in the product. All organic nitrogen fertilizers release nitrogen at different rates. Other nitrogen sources are composted chicken manure, earthworm castings, fish meal, alfalfa meal, feather meal, and canola meal.

Phosphorous
Rock phosphate is a phosphorous additive. This can work well on its own or in combination with bonemeal. Bonemeal and rock phosphate release phosphorous for an entire growing season.

Potash
Kelp meal and greensand are good sources, and so is langbeinite. Crushed granite is good too, but it should be the type that contains a decent supply of potassium feldspar. Greensand releases slowly and for more than a season. Nevertheless, a cup per plant each year is good to add. Kelp has a single-season limitation.

Trace Minerals
There is no substitute for the many trace elements that kelp releases. However, many mined minerals work well too, such as greensand, Pyro Clay™, and Mineral Magic™.

Some liquid organic fertilizers, such as Earth Juice® and Meta Naturals™ have formulas that are made to contain trace elements.

Organic Fertilizer Chart (N=Nitrogen, P=Phosphorous, K=Potash)

Fertilizer	N	P	K
Sea Mix™ 3-2-2	3	2	2
best, all-purpose-water-soluble fertilizer			
alfalfa meal	3	0	2
contains fatty acid, triaconatol, to stimulate growth			
bat guano	2	11	0
can be top-dressed over soil, or dissolved in water			
blood meal	14	0	0
fast and long-acting supply of nitrogen (6 months +)			
bonemeal (steamed)	3	15	0
fast and long-acting source of phosphorous (5 months +)			
canola meal	6	2.5	1
very affordable			
chicken manure (composted)	2	7	2
numbers vary; adds organic matter; makes a good fertilizer tea			
compost	1	1	1
adds organic matter and is a good use of household waste			
cottonseed meal	7	3	2
good amendment for a soil with worm activity			
earthworm castings	5	1	1
acidic; improves soil structure, makes a good fertilizer tea			
Epsom salts	0	0	0
a water-soluble source for magnesium and sulphur			
feather meal	14	0	0
good nitrogen source			
fish and crab meal	8	5	1
trace elements			
fish-bone meal	5	22	1
lots of calcium			
fish emulsion or powder	5 to 12	1 to 2	1 to 2
water soluble			
flaxseed meal	6	3	2
mix into soil			

continues

Organic Fertilizer Chart *continued*

Fertilizer	N	P	K
Flower Power™	4	10	4
an organic blend containing a variety of fertilizers			
granite (crushed)	0	0	8
best with high potassium feldspar content			
greensand	0	1	8
releases potassium for several years			
horn and hoof meal	14	1	0
strong source of nitrogen			
kelp meal	1	1	2
the king of naturally occurring trace minerals			
langbeinite	0	0	22
can be agitated and dissolved for faster availability			
limestone	0	0	0
for calcium, and to neutralize pH of soil / mix			
mushroom manure	1	1	1
adds organic matter and provides many nutrients			
rock phosphate	0	27	0
contains a good supply of calcium			
steer manure	1	1	1
near neutral pH, and adds trace minerals and organic matter			
sunflower hull ash	0	0	44
one of the strongest fast-acting sources of potash available			
Super Grow Mix™	4	4	4
an organic fertilizer mix for general gardening needs			
wood ashes	0	0	8
increases pH, water soluble			

Step 3 : Putting the Mix in the Desired Spot

For an *underground garden*, the mix should be placed into a proper hole. Building a 6-inch to 2-foot raised bed above the hole allows for extra drainage, warmer roots, and more predator control. An option is to apply a manure layer on the bottom of the hole, before the mix is deposited into the hole. For a *container garden*, a grower should fill up the containers and moisten the mix before transplanting. Transplanting is discussed on pages 106 to 107.

Step 4 : Supplemental Fertilization and Watering
Additional liquid, or water-soluble powder fertilizers used at half strength to full strength, are safe additives every week or two.

Chemical Cheat Sheet
Organic fertilizers work well on their own, but they can be used in conjunction with chemical fertilizers.

Many growers use dried and water-soluble organic fertilizers throughout vegetative growth, then switch to chemical fertilizers during bloom.

Another approach is to use a synthetic blend of water-soluble chemical fertilizers during vegetative growth as well. Often a single application of a cheap chemical fertilizer during vegetative growth will push a plant further than no application at all.

All formulas given already in this chapter will work, but here are some more that have done well for plants in vegetative growth or flowering.

Water-Soluble Fertilizers
Vegetative Growth
During vegetative growth, applying one or more applications of a water-soluble chemical fertilizer, such as half to full strength 20-20-20, will produce more vigorous growth. Adding Epsom salts (½-teaspoon per gallon) and the recommended rate of liquid kelp works well with a synthetic chemical blend.

The beauty of adding the odd chemical fertilizer application with the organic mix is that plants do not need these chemicals on a regular basis, since so many other sources of the nutrition are already available. And the odd shot of chemical fertilizer will not build up salts in the soil to the point where reusing the grow medium in the future will give deficient results.

Product quality will not be sacrificed if chemical and organic fertilizers reach a harmonic balance when used together.

Note: Since every part of the world has different environmental conditions, optimal combinations of organic and chemical fertilizers will be different in different areas. For example, in areas of high rainfall, rain leaches the soil every year. In the desert, salts will accumulate.

Studies have shown that in the rainforest, upwards of five chemical fertil-
izations in a single season would not repel earthworms from a mix the following
year. This may not hold true in another location.

Bloom

During bloom, use one to three applications of a water-soluble chemical fertilizer such as Miracle Grow® 15-30-15, Plant Prod™ 15-30-15, General
Hydroponics® Bloom, Supernatural®, Advance Nutrients, or Dyna Bloom™.
The dose can range anywhere from half to full strength. Epsom salts (added at
½-teaspoon per gallon) and the recommended rate of liquid kelp can be added
to the chemical fertilizer, too. Fertilizers should not be added for the last two to
three weeks of blooming. If a grower forgets, plants must get a good flushing to
remove salts in the growing medium no less than a week before harvesting.
Quality will be a borderline issue.

However, flushing with plain water or a flushing solution may be needed to
give the product a final, quality touch, especially for those plants receiving
heavy feedings.

Watering

In addition to supplemental feeding, frequent watering during the hot summer
months may be needed. When the mix feels dry to a depth of 6 to 8 inches or
more in a 1 to 2-foot raised bed or other permanent site, a grower should water
the plants. Container plants will consume different amounts of water for different container sizes. For example, a dry 5-gallon bucket with a plant may need 1
to 5 gallons of water, depending on the situation. Another plant in a dry 20-gal-
lon can may need 5 gallons but prefer 10 gallons. Plants that receive a good supply of water grow better.

There are many possibilities for dealing with the water supply; for example,
a gravity feeding unit, a portable electric pump, black plastic water traps, water
drums, a solar pump, a gas water-pumping system, or a well. A sprinkler system
can be attached to a flowing water supply.

Another approach is to cover a plant site with a thick layer of straw, bark,
weed-free hay, sphagnum peat moss (if available at the site), black plastic, or
wood chips, all of which help retain moisture in the mix. One grower placed a
45-gallon drum in a flowing body of water and connected a series of tubing that

became gradually narrower, resulting in a lot of pressure buildup in the line, which forced the water uphill to the site.

Burying buckets and garbage bags instead of exposing them will cut back dramatically on watering maintenance, especially in moist areas.

Placing a Myco Pak under each plant at transplanting time seems to lower watering needs.

It is critical that a grower understand the direct and overlapping relationships between strain, timing of transplant, quality of mix, and container size, to mention only a few issues. A grower should get his feet in the water to get a grip on these realities.

Placing the garden in a moist location is the easist and cheapest way to grow a low-maintenance garden.

Step 5: Flushing Out Fertilizer

When procedures in this manual are followed, the final product should be of top quality. However, flushing plants with lots of plain water two weeks before harvest and upwards until harvest can remove lots of salts. This flushing will improve the final product. In general, these formulas with organic mixes should work out fine without the need for flushing, unless many supplemental feedings are added. A major benefit of organic fertilizer use, is that salts are not a by-product of organic fertilizers, unlike chemical fertilizers, especially the cheap ones. Flushing is often more necessary for chemically grown plants, so that the outcome is produce of a higher quality. In most cases, using too many chemical fertilizers will affect the final quality if they are not flushed out of the mix. If making one to five applications of chemical fertilizer in a single season during vegetative growth and the flowering process, the mix will not deal with the detrimental levels of salt buildup, even without doing a serious flush.

Nevertheless, adding a few doses of chemical fertilizer during cultivation can increase the volume, without sacrifice to quality.

If flushing is necessary, using large amounts of plain water or one of the many flushing formulas available in the market today is recommended. These flushing formulas attach to the fertilizer salts and unused elements in the growing medium so that they will be removed. Some clearing solutions come in flavors like pina colada and strawberry. Some flushing formulas should be followed up with a dose of plain water in order to remove an undesirable flavor.

Step 6: Reusing Soilless Mix and Forest Compost

When the indoor or outdoor crop is finished, the mix can be reused, meaning that the grow medium can be used over and over again. This is beneficial, because after each crop is done, the grow mix retains its investment value, since it can be reused indefinitely. The chart shows how mix volume increases year in and year out. Only new fertilizers need to be added for each additional grow shown.

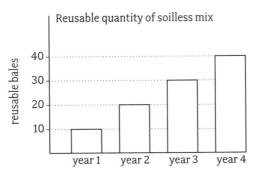

Reusing soilless mix allows a garden size to multiply.

All organic nitrogen sources, such as blood meal, fish meal, feather meal, earthworm castings, chicken manure, and canola meal are effective for a single outdoor growing season. Phosphorous needs to be replenished each year. Bonemeal and rock phosphate work well independently or as a combination.

Mineral potash sources such as greensand and crushed granite extended their usefulness beyond a single season. The minerals will break down slowly over time, releasing potash to the roots. Fast-acting potash, good for a single season, is available in kelp meal and wood ashes. Kelp meal also provides most of the necessary trace minerals for the plant. Adding Epsom salts when watering adds magnesium and sulphur.

Grow mix is best reused outdoors, because the outdoor environment harbors a different balance than an indoor climate. If indoor mix is not treated with a good dose of 35% hydrogen peroxide (2 to 5ml per gallon) or calcium peroxide in between crops, plants will be more susceptible to disease. If grow mix is reused indoors, a peroxide treatment is a must, or the leaves may develop strange-looking rusts or growths from the contaminated mix.

Grow medium can harbor root disease that thrives in the indoor climate. If the mix is moved outside and dug into the earth, the balance in the natural environment will take over. Reused indoor mix that has shown root disease and harbored excessive mite populations can be transferred outdoors to grow large, healthy plants. The outdoor balance is different, and a strong, acclimatized strain can thrive there and fight off any negative properties, such as root fungus, that may exist in the mix.

Nevertheless, when growing outdoors, a poor quality mix and a weak strain often promote other problems. For example, a weak strain may develop leaf spot fungus, while a plant growing next to it in the same mix will be totally healthy. Another example is that of two identical cloned plants grown side by side outdoors in the same mix. One plant fertilized often in 20 gallons of mix may thrive, while the other plant with no fertilizer applications in 1 gallon of mix is serious bug dinner.

Using hydrogen peroxide (H_2O_2) definitely reduces potential problems when the mix is reused indoors. H_2O_2 will shed an oxygen molecule to form water and atomic oxygen. Oxygen on its own will destroy anaerobic bacteria and viruses as well as provide oxygen to the roots.

Here is a list of many reusing techniques for outdoor cultivation. These methods should be done one month before transplanting, but if preparation and transplanting happen on the same day, results will be more than sufficient.

Method 1

This method uses containers that are 5 to 20 gallons. For garbage cans, a 12-inch (30cm) hole should be cut in each bottom. Then a screen is stapled into the bottom from the inside of container. Garbage bags with holes in the bottoms also work.

Perlite and / or half a bag of steer manure can be used to make a layer (1 to 4 inches) on the container bottoms. The manure layer is the ticket.

The used mix (about one 4.0 cubic feet bale's worth) can be laid onto some sort of tarp while removing all roots and stalks. Mixing on a tarp, in a large bin, or in a cement mixer makes it possible for thorough combining of all the materials. The next step is adding one bag of composted steer manure, one 9kg bag of earthworm castings, one 5kg bag of Welcome Harvest Farm™ Flower Power™, and 3 cups of fine dolomite lime. Adding ⅓ to ½ part soil (pH near 7 is best) stretches the cost.

Adding perlite, sand, vermiculite, and calcium peroxide (i.e. Grotek™ Oxycal or Soil Blaster™) are customizing options to give plant roots more air.

Garbage bag bud.

Perlite and sand allow water to drain well, while vermiculite holds water. Calcium peroxide is purchased in a powdered form and gives a slow release of oxygen and will also break down to form lime.

Another option is to use any recipe from pages 61 to 63.

After the mix is thoroughly combined, the garbage cans or bags should be filled and placed outside at the site in the spring. If the mix will be left longer than two months, a grower should place a cover over the mix in order to prevent the fertilizers from leaching, which is wasteful. If rainfall will be low for the area, then it is possible to prepare sites earlier without adding a cover.

Plants during vegetative growth should be fine without additional fertilizer, but a grower can apply the odd half full-strength application of a fertilizer for marijuana plants.

For alternative feeding methods, there is the chemical cheat sheet on pages

67, 97 or the organic hydroponic recipes on pages 97 to 103, and hydroponic formulas on pages 95 to 96.

Mix should never be allowed to dry, which will cause the plants to wilt. Remember that giving a heavy dose of water in the middle of the day can give the plants a mild shock, especially if the water is from a lake, spring, or glacial melt.

Technical

Water should be at pH 6.0 to 6.6 during vegetative growth, and at 5.5 to 6.4 during flowering. The temperature should be around 70°F. Roots obtain nutrients more effectively when the temperature fits their needs.

Watering with cold water (below 70°F) in the cooler parts of the day goes more with the flow of the root temperature, because it will heat up during the part of the day when growth is most productive. Photosynthesis will slow down when light levels lessen, and therefore watering is best at that time, so it can saturate the mix and be utilized for the next productive daylight time.

Production can be taken further by maintaining a warm root temperature, around 70°F, during darkness, to allow plants to make a more solid root system. Adding sand to the mix can raise the root temperature. Highly productive hydroponicists maintain this constant root temperature for their plants.

Method 2

Taking all the mix to a sunny, safe site with a somewhat decent water supply is a good way to start. A 2-foot square hole should be dug about 1-foot deep. Holes can be smaller, but they should be no less than 10 to 12 inches in diameter. It is best to estimate the potential production of the strain to make an accurate and nonwasteful-sized hole.

Rocks, metal fencing covered in thick black plastic, or wood can be used to build a raised bed 1 to 2 feet high. Spreading one bag of manure on the bottom of the raised bed gives a definite edge, because it allows for a meal later on when the roots reach it. The next step is to dump a bunch of old mix (about one bale's worth or 4.0 cubic feet) into the bed. Then it is recommended to add one bag of composted steer manure, 3 cups of fine dolomite lime, 3 cups of blood meal, 6 cups of bonemeal, 3 cups of greensand, 3 cups of kelp meal, and one-third part soil. The soil can be sandy, clay-like, boggy, forest compost, or topsoil. Ideally, the overall pH will be about 6.0 to 6.5. All materials should be mixed well with a claw, a pitchfork, in a cement mixer, or wearing gloves to keep the hands clean and smell-free.

Adding a material that gives more air to the roots will boost yield by a significant percentage. Perlite or sand will give extra drainage and add more air to the grow medium. Vermiculite will give the mix more air and increase its water-holding capacity. Calcium peroxide is a powdered material that will break down into oxygen and lime. It can be added any time to fine-tune the texture.

It is critical when mixing all products not to disturb the manure layer that lines the bottom.

During budding, any (half to full) recommended rate of a commercial product is effective. Plants should be watered generously during hot periods, with amounts that will saturate the mix well.

For other fertilizing methods, there are references in the chemical cheat sheet on pages 61 to 63, or organic hydroponic formulas on pages 97 to 103.

Technical

The water should be pH 6.0 to 6.6 during vegetative growth and 5.5 to 6.3 during bloom. The temperature should be around 70°F. At least one 9 to 15-foot stake will be needed to support a healthy, high-yielding plant strain in this mix. It is not too much for one plant!

Method 3

Other cultivation options are the use of either garbage cans, other containers, or the 2-foot square site. The first step is to thoroughly mix about one 4.0 cubic feet bale's worth of old mix with one bag of steer manure.

Another bag of steer manure lining the bottom of a can or hole is important for success. Using one bag of composted steer manure in a hole, or half a bag in a 20-gallon container, allows two bucks to go a long way. Now a plant can be transplanted into the mix.

A grower can supplementally feed every week, or every second week with any commercial product designed for flowering plants. The fertilizing application can be at a rate of half to full strength. Other feeding possibilities are described in earlier in this chapter 3 with hydroponic and organic hydroponic formulas that will work well. The chemical cheat sheet on pages 61 to 63 shows more feeding methods with inorganic plant food.

These fertilizing techniques are very similar to those of the indoor program. All mixes should be soaked well during dry conditions. On a regular basis, applying ten gallons or more of solution per plant in the peak of summer may be necessary for plants in garbage cans, especially in heavy-sunlight areas.

To feed plants from the water source while making life simpler, the following watering items may be used: a rechargeable battery pack with a 300-gallon-per-hour pump attached via a DC-to-AC inverter, a solar pump, or a portable gas pump. All that is needed is a fertilizer-mixing unit attached to a garden hose. A direct feed from the end of a hose or a capped hose end with ¼-inch lines going to various plant sites does the job.

Method 4

One more option worth trying is the one-third compost trip. In this case, one to two parts of decomposed compost are added to two parts of the reusable mix. Cheap and light perlite, sand, vermiculite, or calcium peroxide can be added later to allow for more aeration to the plant roots. Perlite and sand allow for better drainage, and vermiculite holds water.

Extreme Outdoor Hydroponic Systems

The systems in this chapter are designed to deal with all predators, domestic and wild. These predators can cause problems for novices and experienced gardeners alike. Since animals such as dogs, cougars, and bears like to bite on tubing (and other man-made objects), it is advised to make systems that they cannot tamper with. These systems can be of value to a homesteader or a country farmer that is exposed to such predators.

We have already discussed fertilizing earlier in this chapter. Any commercial product used at the recommended rate works. Now we will look at hydroponic feeding in greater detail. A grower should know how to feed hydroponically in order to grow a successful crop in a hydroponic system.

Rule #1

A grower should try to grow with a local medium. The natural surroundings may contain materials like fir bark, granitic sand (.6mm to 2mm; ¹⁄₁₆-inch in size), granitic gravel (1.5mm to 2.0cm; less than ³⁄₄ in size), hemlock sawdust, peat moss, or dolomite sand (which shifts pH and contains calcium and magnesium).

It makes no sense spending a fortune on materials and transportation to a farm site, if quality hydroponic mediums are there in the first place. Most commercial hydroponic farms use materials that are available nearby.

After noting what materials are available nearby, the grower should consider what type of system to build in order to make use of the growing medium.

For example, a grower in a controlled environment such as a greenhouse, may wish to implement a top-feeding system using a medium that allows the roots to get sufficient oxygen and nutrition, such as clay, sawdust, fir bark, perlite, or perlite / sand.

On the other hand, a grower in a wild country setting may rather use local granitic sand opposed to local granitic gravel. If sand is used, a one-way system can be implemented easily if plants are fed intermittently with a solar-powered pump. Sand that is fed at the proper rate will not have too much runoff waste, and therefore a recirculating system is not necessary. But if gravel is used, the solution will drain more rapidly, thus a recovery system must be used or a giant reservoir must be utilized so that plants don't dry up.

Rule #2

A grower should use a system that will give a reasonable yield with easy maintenance.

For example, if a grower decides to set up a commercial farm on property where many wild animals live, such as bears, deer, cougars, etc., then a hydroponic system where all the feeding materials are buried underground may be necessary in order to keep the plants alive. Many snoopy animals may examine a man-made obstacle, yet they tend not to make a serious mess of a non-food source. Tubing exposed above the ground will probably get chewed on, thus leaving holes in unwanted areas which can lead to solution going to the wrong places.

Bottom-Feeding

A good system that can be used anywhere would be one in which large beds or trenches are built, 1 to 2 feet wide and up to 3 feet deep, depending on the crop and the time of planting. The beds or trenches should be lined with 1 to 2 sheets of 6ml black plastic, followed by PVC pipe buried at the bottom; next, top up the beds or trench with the growing medium. Beds or trenches should have a small slope so that solution drains down the bottom. A 1-inch slope for every 4 to 8 feet works, allowing the solution to drain freely out of one end, or to drain back into the reservoir and be recirculated. Holes should be made in the bottom of the PVC pipe for solution to escape into the growing medium so that bottom-feeding is possible. Some PVC drain pipe comes with holes in the pipe, thus saving a step of work. The diameter of the pipe depends on the flow rate going through the pipe. 1 to 3-inch pipe will do the trick.

It is possible to use smaller diameter PVC pipe, or polybutylene tubing. In this case a grower may want to put more than one piece of pipe in each trench, or place them close together in a bed.

All the PVC should be end capped so that solution is forced through the holes.

The flow rate being pumped through the pipe will be the more important factor in determining spacing than the diameter of the pipe. And, PVC under 1-inch is often substantially cheaper than the larger sizes. Also, as PVC increases in diameter, so does its thickness, therefore weight is another factor to consider, especially if moving the PVC for long distances is part of the program.

If predators are not a problem, plants can be top-fed instead of bottom-fed. Top-feedings helps against salts building up, as opposed to bottom-feeding methods. Bottom-fed plants should get flushed periodically unless a good percentage of the fertilizing formula is organic, with a low salt count.

A grower can never go wrong with 1 to 2 days of flushing with plain water per week. Even though that can be overdoing it in some cases, a grower may want to be more safe than sorry.

The Drain to Waste System

A drain to waste system is basically a drip-watering system where a fertilized solution is used but not recirculated. Making a drip-watering system has been described on pages 52 to 56. Basically, any medium can be used, even the local dirt supply. Hopefully the medium has some air-holding capabilities. Sand, perlite, gravel, sawdust, vermiculite, peat moss, soilless mix, or calcium peroxide can be added to give more air-holding capabilities.

Calcium peroxide is the most portable way to oxygenate roots in soil or soilless mediums. Calcium peroxide has a 6-week life. PH of the medium should be 4.0 to 6.5. The pH of the solution is more important. A vegetating growth formula should be at 6.0 to 6.6 during vegetative growth and up to the first 2 weeks of flowering, and, then 5.5 to 6.3 during the duration of flowering. Parts per million should be 1,000 to 1,500PPM.

A good gravity system or tap can be used to get the water to the plants.

Tubing that is buried will be better protected from animals. However, frequent checks are important because there are curious animals that notice new objects in their territory. If a system is top-fed, the header line carrying the solution to the plants should be buried. Feeder lines can be attached to the underground header line and drawn to the top of the growing medium for top-feeding. If a predator does damage in this case, then solution will still drain out damaged parts so that plants can still get solution.

The diagram in this section shows a drip system too.

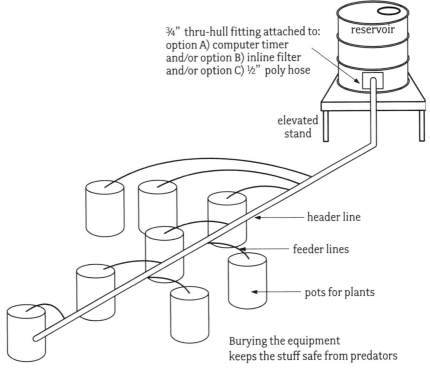

¾" thru-hull fitting attached to:
option A) computer timer
and/or option B) inline filter
and/or option C) ½" poly hose

reservoir

elevated
stand

header line

feeder lines

pots for plants

Burying the equipment
keeps the stuff safe from predators

Uncomplicated representation of a drip system.

Outdoor NFT
Making Trenches
The first step is to dig a 6-inch to 2-foot trench in the dirt. The dirt should be sturdy, such as hardpan or clay.

The second step is to use two or more layers of black poly to coat the bottom of the trench.

On top of the black poly, any medium can be used to support the plants such as clay, sawdust, rockwool, river stones, granite, or fir bark. The width and depth of the channel depends on several factors, such as how big the plants are to be grown.

However, 2 to 3 gallons of medium easily can be used to grow a 6x6-foot plant. More can be used for huge plants, but staking may be more to deal with than it is worth.

If a gravel or clay that absorbs ions is used, it needs to be flushed almost as often as plants are fed.

Feeding for 4 to 5 days and flushing with plain water for 2 days is a plan that can be implemented from start to finish, or when plants begin to intake lots of food. This plan can be used for all growing mediums.

The trenches can receive solution pumped upward from the reservoir, or downward with a drain to waste from a high reservoir. If the system is not recirculating, it is best to have a slow water flow that effectively moves down the trench in order to keep the fertilizer costs to a minimum. An absorbent medium on the bottom of the NFT channel can help to hold more water and more plant food. Solution is delivered from the reservoir to the trenches with gravity, or with a pump.

Reservoir
If the ground is hard and only a negligible amount of water is lost to the ground, then the reservoir may need no liner (i.e. swimming pool liner or black poly plastic). A reservoir can be low maintenance if it can get a slow refill of ground water, or water from another source.

Fertilizer can be manually added to the reservoir, or an in-line fertilzer can be used. In-line fertilizer is available at garden centers and hydroponic stores.

Growing in Soil
Step 1: Finding and Preparing Quality Dirt
Quality dirt should be loosened with a shovel, pitchfork, claw, or rototiller. Then, if hand tools are used, a hole or a trench should be dug. The dirt should be placed in a pile with the stones removed. Placing a 1 to 2-inch layer of steer manure in the bottom of the hole or trench is recommended for the future roots. Soil tests can be made with inexpensive soil test kits available at garden centers. If tests

Quality dirt + quality preparation + quality feeding = quality bud.

are made, it is recommended to keep a log in order to reference how well a technique works in specific dirt.

Deciduous canopies such as alder trees often have good dirt, as do many riverbanks, areas where a river has overflowed and pushed the dirt away, arable farmland, and old quality gardens. Creek beds often contain a good dirt supply. Certain plant species reveal the quality of dirt beneath them, or they can reveal how easy a site is to prepare. Grassy areas often indicate a potential garden site.

Good dirt compacts when it is squeezed, then crumbles when it is broken up. Soils like this often hold decent moisture. Sandy soils won't compact too well.

The next step is to put the aerated, fine dirt back into the hole. An option is to add more quality dirt to create a raised site, which allows for better drainage, or dirt can be put in a container (of 2 to 20 gallons).

Drainage at the site is an important factor. Poor drainage can be good in a very dry environment, yet be devastating in a rainforest. Fast drainage can cause

This dirt garden with cannabis and desert plants is a pleasure to the eyes.

overworking, which is why peat moss is so good. It holds water and nutrients much more effectively than soil, and it drains well. When peat is saturated, decent oxygen is still available to the plant's roots, so that feeding can be effective. The grower must put two and two together at this point. Some soils drain so quickly that watering may be needed several times a week. Knowledge of dirt's capabilities helps determine what the workload will be during the grow season.

Inevitably, the plant strain plays a large role in determining the drainage needs. For example, if the area of cultivation is dry for the whole growing season, the drainage factor is easy to know. However, if the rains come on in the autumn, a strain that finishes before the rain means less drainage is needed. But a strain that finishes in the rains needs good drainage and a decent supply of oxygen, and of course mold-resistance. Often, soils that drain poorly during adverse weather can bring on a mold problem as opposed to a grow medium that drains well and is not choked up from puddles of water.

Step 2: Liming
A grower can add fine dolomite lime 4 to 6 months before transplanting for the first season at the new site. A grower should apply and thoroughly mix the lime until the dirt pH hits near neutral (pH 7.0). Cheap test kits are available from garden centers to determine this. This is probably an investment worth making until the exact quantities of lime needed for the particular dirt type are determined. Dolomite lime has a neutral pH and makes this step a piece of cake. Adding it early is important to neutralize the pH, so that calcium and other elements can be utilized later during the grow season. It takes a few months for dolomite to break down and become available to the plants.

Step 3: Adding Material to Improve the Soil
Sand, perlite, peat moss, or vermiculite can now be added and evenly mixed to loosen and aerate the soil. Perlite will allow water to drain well and is therefore beneficial for a wetter soil. Vermiculite will hold water and is good for a drier soil. Sand will help heat the soil and is good for a wetter soil type, as it loosens up the dirt and allows for decent drainage. Peat holds water, air, and nutrient. Adding ½ peat moss and ⅓ parts perlite is a good addition to give the roots air, and to retain moisture and nutrient.

Step 4: Adding Fertilizer
A soil test is made with a soil test kit, or by taking a sample to a garden center for testing to determine levels of nitrogen, phosphorous, and potassium.

Option A: Organic Fertilizers
However, adding and thoroughly mixing 1 cup of blood meal, 2 cups of bonemeal, 1 cup of greensand, and 1 cup of kelp meal per plant is a safe combination to deliver the food supply until the buds are in bloom. Optimal fertilizer amounts for specific dirt will require improvisation, because sandy soils don't hold nutrients as effectively as peat or clay soils. The dried fertilizers can be added a few months prior to transplanting if thick, black plastic is used to cover the site to protect it from rain, which breaks down the dried fertilizers. The dried fertilizers can be added any time before transplanting, even on the same day. Soilless mix recipes can be used from pages 61 to 63 but, because all dirt is different, there are no guarantees. This is work to figure out the specifics.

This backyard bud was fed and flushed just right. The juicy buds and yellowing of leaves are telltale signs.

Organic matter such as a half a bag of composted steer manure (very cheap) per plant can be added to the soil as well.

The site can be flat to the ground or it can be a raised bed.

During vegetative growth and flowering, more food may be needed. Supplemental feedings are described in pages 67 to 68. Alternately, any recommended rate of a commercial fertilizer designed for flowering plants applied at half of full strength will work fine.

Option B: Using Slow-Release Chemical Fertilizers

Slow-release chemical fertilizers can be purchased with or without a protective osmocote. Fertilizers of this type can release over time periods such as 3 months, 6 months, 1 year, etc.

It is recommended to use a time release that stops expelling the fertilizer before the harvest date, so that excessive fertilizer release does not spoil the bud quality. Slow-release fertilizers come in all sorts of fancy numbers such as 6-8-6, 7-7-7, and 14-14-14. These particular numbers will work out quite fine.

Normally, a small handful is all that is needed to grow a hefty plant. Note that using too much can lead to plant burning: in this case plant leaves will curl over and many leaves will become brown and crispy.

During vegetative growth and flowering, more plant food may be needed. Any recommended rate of a commercial fertilizer applied at half of full strength works fine. A grower should not fertilize for the two weeks prior harvest.

Hydroponic / Aeroponic / Organic Soil Feeding
How to Mix a Nutrient Solution
Mixing a nutrient solution can be as easy as doing what the fertilizer bottle says to apply. Most fertilizers' recommended rates normally give a decent supply of the nutrients a plants needs. However, some are definitely better than others and are more specific to a specific plant's needs. Brands such as Greenfire® Earth Juice, Welcome Harvest Farm™, General Hydroponics®, Advance Nutrients®, Supernatural®, and others all give formulas for growing in soil, soilless, and hydroponic systems.

On the other hand, fertilizing can be made into a science depending on what the grower is trying to achieve. Some growers like to gain complete control over all the elements by customizing their formulas to particular feeding needs during all stages of growth. Determining the feeding needs of a particular strain is another important factor in working out a proper feeding formula so that a grower can give optimum nutrition and save costs.

It is possible to determine the parts per million (PPM) of a particular element such as nitrogen from the percentages of the elements listed on the fertilizer package.

Calculating Parts per Million
A chemical-fertilized nutrient solution should be at 1,000 to 1,500PPM to be on the safe side in most cases, but custom adjustments (i.e. 800PPM) can be made depending upon the plant. A TDS meter will give a reading in PPM (parts per million). Expensive meters measure a large span of elements and can be used to keep all feeding costs to the bare minimum because specific nutrients can be added when specific nutrients are used by the plants.

An organic, or a chemical-organic fertilized nutrient solution should be no higher than 1,500PPM. With an organic or a chemical-organic solution, a grower

Buds are in nice shape and the leaves are turning yellow prior to harvest. These factors are a sign of proper feeding.

can push the quantity of certain elements because a lot of the fertilizer will not contain salts that hinder growth when they are in a solution in excess. For example, when Earth Juice® Grow and Earth Juice® Bloom are used to obtain the desired PPM of nitrogen and calcium, the PPM on a meter would be lower than if a solution of calcium nitrate was used to give the same PPM of nitrogen and calcium.

There will be dissolved solids in an organic hydroponic system from sources such as bat guano, Epsom salts (magnesium sulphate), sulphate of potash, humic acid, etc. However, some fertilizers will add nutrients but the PPM meter will not fluctuate. In a nutshell, this is the advantage of many organic fertilizers: no toxic salts. Results will be excellent if an organic solution is changed weekly, every 10 days, or every second week with a good fertilizing formula. A solution can go unchanged for longer periods of time with additions of new nutrients from time to time, especially when plants are small and don't feed as much. However, since plant nutrient requirements are always changing and some nutrient deficiencies are hard to detect, it is advised to change the solution regularly to save the hassle of determining what plant food is needed, and when. Also, just because plants are green doesn't mean that they are growing at maximum production.

Monitoring a Hydroponic / Aeroponic Reservoir
Young Plants
Young plants tend to use more water than nutrient. Therefore, for the first 2 to 4 weeks, adding plain water to a reservoir is probably all that is needed, because solution will become saline (i.e. 1,800PPM) when a plant takes in water without much nutrient. Until plants start to use a decent amount of nutrient, it is not necessary to do complete reservoir changes because there are nutrients that have not been used by the plants. In most cases, 600 to 1,000PPM is adequate for seedlings and vegetative growth.

Aging Plants
It doesn't hurt to make a solution on the weak side (i.e. 1,000PPM) until plants start to use equal parts nutrient and water, because PPM will rise as water is used by the plants.

When plants use equal parts nutrient and water, adding 1,000 to 1,500PPM concentrated solution is recommended.

When plants use more nutrient than water, adding a concentrated solution about 1,500PPM is recommended, unless a stronger concentration is needed to keep PPM at optimal levels. One should try to keep the PPM near 1,500PPM in the reservoir when liquid is added. This way, the solution will stay within the 1,000 to 1,500PPM boundaries, even as PPM slowly drops as plants use more nutrient than water.

When a reservoir needs changing (i.e. every 1 to 2 weeks), it is a good idea to allow the solution to run low. For example, if a full reservoir is at 1,500PPM, it is possible to allow water and nutrient to lower to a level such as 800PPM. This will give a little flush since the solution is a little on the weak side. And now there is only a little liquid to pump out of the reservoir before a new solution is added, thus minimizing maintenance.

A major factor worth noting is that larger reservoirs will have less fluctuations in PPM and pH and will keep maintenance down.

Two gallons of solution per plant in a top-feeding system is a good amount to put in a reservoir. This size compensates only for minor daily fluctuations in PPM and pH.

Plants that are close to intense light will use nutrient up more quickly than plants that receive less intense light.

When plants do not get the correct doses of food, nutrient deficiencies occur. When a deficiency occurs, plants normally change color from green to green-yellow to yellow. Deficiencies are often a sign that the reservoir needs a change, or specific elements need to be added to the reservoir.

When a deficiency occurs, it is recommended to give the plants the food they crave (i.e. nitrogen or calcium). Nitrogen is the most common deficiency.

Deficiencies should change within a day or two after the proper fertilizer is applied, and plants should go back to a healthy green, unless the deficiency caused serious damage.

How to Use and Clean a TDS Meter

A. The TDS meter electrodes should be rinsed with clean or distilled water, or isopropyl alcohol and water. A Q-tip helps scrub the electrodes free of debris.

B. Now the meter should be submersed in a calibrating solution (ie. 1,000PPM). A small container or the protective cap around the electrodes serves as a place to hold the calibrating solution.

C. The dial should be turned until the reading shows that of the calibrating solution (i.e. 1,000PPM).

D. The electrodes should then be cleaned again with clean or distilled water.

E. The meter should be dipped in the reservoir after the fertilizer is added.

F. Fertilizer (chemical fertilizers) or water should be added to adjust
the reading between 1,000 to 1,500PPM.

If the PPM is higher than wanted, adding water can dilute the solution to the desired PPM range. The meter is actually useless in determining proper amounts of an organic or chemical-organic solution, but it is a good reference meter. There is a section in this chapter showing organic formulations and chemical formulations, and a section showing how to get the desired PPM of a specific element (i.e. nitrogen) in a fertilizer on pages 88 to 90.

Hopefully the water source is near 0PPM so that water is not stocked with unwanted PPM that can put limits on the amount of fertilizer added to a solution. There are many relatively inexpensive machines such as reverse osmosis machines and distillation devices that remove unwanted dissolved solids from a water supply.

Note: The PPM readings should only be used as a reference as to when to change solutions because they do not read the actual parts per million of a solution. Calculating parts per million of a particular fertilizer or element is best done with a little math and chemistry calculation as explained on pages 88 to 90.

Most meters are priced under $100. These measure PPM on a scale of 100 (i.e. 100, 500, 1000, 1100). For most people, these meters do the deed. However, there are expensive meters that measure a wide variety of elements in a solution. These tools are for an experienced hydroponic farmer.

Determining PPM without a Meter
Step 1
The percentage of the elements in a fertilizer (i.e. 20-20-20) is needed in order to determine the PPM.

The fertilizer packs are listed as NPK. N is all nitrogen, but phosphorous is listed as a compound (P_2O_5), and potassium is listed as (K_2O).

Phosphorous (P) is 44% of phosphoric acid (P_2O_5), potassium (K) is 83% of potash (K_2O).

To get the PPM from a 15-30-15 fertilizer, the first step is to take all three numbers and move the decimal one decimal place over to the right. In the case of nitrogen, the number would be 200. This number will give the parts per mil-

Marijuana leaves can often explain a situation. For example, green marijuana leaves with no leaf curl show quality growth, whereas light green or yellowing leaves and red or purplish veins running down each blade shows that the plant is nutrient deficient.

Bud and sun: a perfect match.

Nice colas in this well-maintained garden.

The pink pistils protruding from this pot parallel the color of clover.

Bud potency will increase until the bud is mature.

These buds have been pollinated to form hard seeds.

Buds require plenty of sun, food, and water in order to grow to a large size, especially during the middle of flowering.

Cold, autumn weather can hinder growth. Red leaves and small buds are a common result in these weather conditions.

A hidden location is chosen.

Area for the garden is cleared.

Manure bags are opened and ready to add to the soil.

Soil is dug up, turned, and loosened.

Manure is added to the soil.

The garden plot is well camouflaged and receives plenty of sun.

Plants are transplanted into the soil.

Cannabis plant growing in a mobile grow bag.

The base of the pot plant in contact with the dirt.

Small, decorative plant is flowering in a clay pot.

Plants will live fine, but might need support when the roots get exposed in grow bags as the mix compresses or bags expand.

Buds were manicured while the plant was still growing in the earth.

Upward growing fan leaves are a genetic trait.

Late flowering bud in front of the setting sun.

Plants have been successfully transplanted into the prepared site.

These ganja plants in vegetative growth are thriving in the garden.

On any healthy plant, the odd severely yellowed leaf, colored dying leaf, or crispy brown dead leaf can be picked off and discarded.

Plant pistils can appear in several colors, including white, red, orange, pink, and purple.

Poor weather and lack of time can give low yields and poor quality on any strain.

Cold weather and colored leaves indicate the end of the outdoor marijuana plant's lifecycle.

Growers must know which bugs do damage in the specific growing area and how to control them.

Spiders can make webs and gather insects, but they do not harm the marijuana plant.

Bud mold can attack small and large sections of the plant.

Leaves that develop mildew, mold and other residue problems should be picked from the plants and / or sprayed with a fungicide to minimize further damage.

Plant diseases can leave all kinds of rusty marks, strange colors and holes in the leaves.

The undersides of leaves can be a hang out for predators like mites and caterpillars.

Contaminated soil, a weak strain, poor feeding, and uncontrolled predators can cause problems that get out of hand.

Outdoor raised beds can be made with scraps of wood found in the bush.

Clones or seedlings can be transplanted to the outdoor site in a disposable cardboard box.

Nitrogen deficiency starts with yellowing of the older leaves—located towards the bottom of the plant—and works its way up.

Hoophouses extend the growing season and protect plants, while climate controlled greenhouses can give the best conditions for outdoor marijuana cultivation.

Small plants are very simple to maintain because they do not require training or large amounts of water.

Small, healthy plants rarely require any staking for support.

Large, budding plants cultivated in rows are given help for support.

This grower is pleased to see his tall, vigorous plant.

Lots of space for this outdoor garden.

This plant has leaves with 5 to 11 blades, which indicates normal growth. Although it is not uncommon, when plants break out in patterns of 1 to 3 blades per leaf something has usually gone wrong.

Drip irrigation helped produce around a couple of ounces of bud from this plant.

Feeder line is attached to the stake to keep it in position.

This weed is growing directly out of a sack.

Leaves are changing color on this late flowering plant, indicating that harvest is right around the corner.

Young clones are ready for a good place to grow.

lion of nitrogen when 1 gram is added to each quart or liter.

For phosphorous, a grower should multiply the 300 by .44. For example, 300 x .44 = 132PPM.This number will give the parts per million of phosphorous when 1 gram is added to each quart or liter.

For potassium, a grower should multiply the 150 by .83. For example, 150 x .83 = 124.5PPM. This number will give the parts per million of potassium when 1 gram is added to each quart or liter.

More Advanced Note: Some growers make their own plant food with 5 to 7 basic salts, as described on pages 95 to 96.

How to get the percentage of an element (i.e. K = potassium) in a compound (i.e. K_2SO_4).

Here is how to get desired parts per million of sulphur (S) and potassium (K) in potassium sulphate (K_2SO_4).

A. The periodic table of elements should be referenced in order to get the atomic numbers of each atom. For example, potassium has an atomic number of 19, sulphur has an atomic number of 16, and oxygen has an atomic number of 8.

B. Now, to determine the percentage of each element, all the elements must have their atomic numbers multiplied by the number of ions in a compound. In the case of K_2SO_4, the atomic number of potassium, which is 19, is multiplied by 2 to give 38, because there are 2 potassium ions. Since there is only one sulphur ion, 16 is multiplied by 1 to give 16. Oxygen has 4 ions in the compound, therefore 8 is multiplied by 4 to give 32.

C. Now all of the atomic numbers are multiplied by the number of ions, then all of the atoms multiplied by their atomic weights are added up. For example, the total number in potassium sulphate is (2 x 19) +16 + (4x 8) = 86.

D. To get the percentage of each element, the amount of ions is multiplied by the element's atomic number. For example, in the case of potassium, 2 x 19 = 38.

E. The amount of ions multiplied by the element's atomic number is divided by the sum of all the elements multiplied by their atomic numbers. In the case of potassium, the 38 (number of ions x atomic number) is divided by 86 = .44.

F. The number multiplied by 100 gives the percentage. For potassium, .44 x 100 = 44%.

Step 2
Finally, the percentage number should have the decimal place moved over one place to the right. In the case of potassium, the number would be 440. This number will give the parts per million of an element when 1 gram is added to each quart or liter. In the case of potassium , 1 gram of potassium sulphate in a quart of liquid will give 440PPM of potassium. Using half a gram per quart will give 220PPM of potassium and 95PPM of Sulphur.

Available PPM
The level of solubility (and purity) in water will make the final say. For example, some solutions and powders will completely dissolve into usable ions, while others will not be soluble in water, hence the elements will not be readily available to plants. For example, gypsum ($CaSO_4$) is not very soluble in water, which makes it almost useless for hydroponic usage. However, gypsum does break down slowly in soil where it works fine. All formulas in this chapter are nearly 100% soluble in water.

How to pH a Solution
PH is the measure of the hydrogen ion concentration in a solution or other medium. There are more hydrogen ions in an acid solution than in a basic solution. On a scale, a pH of 7.0 is neutral, under 7.0 is acidic, and over 7.0 is alkaline. A plant's intake of certain elements is greatly affected by pH. A pH of 5.5 to 6.5 is the standard for this organic hydroponic technique. A pH of 6.0 to 6.5 works well for vegetative growth and early flowering, while a pH of 5.5 to 6.3 works well during flowering.

A. The pH of plain water should be checked before adding the fertilizers. That pH number should be written down where it can easily be found. If the water pH is the same in the future, it is easier to make a quick formula using the same fertilizers without having to measure.

B. All of the fertilizers can be added and mixed well. The quantities should be written down for future reference.

C. A clean pH pen should be calibrated at 7.0, which is the pH reading of the calibrating solution.

D. The pen should be dipped into the solution and pH up or pH down should be added until the reading is in the preferred 5.5 to 6.5 range.

Examples of organic pH up are baking soda (sodium bicarbonate), Earth Juice® Natural Up and wood ashes. There are endless pH up solutions available anywhere garden supplies are available. Baking soda should be used carefully, because too much sodium is not wanted. Fortunately, sodium can be flushed out with plain water. The plants can absorb improper amounts of sodium if the potassium levels are not sufficient. Using feeding combinations that don't rock the pH level means little or no pH up is needed.

An example of organic pH down is the addition of Earth Juice® Natural Down, and Greenfire® Earth Juice Grow. White flour and vinegar have been reported to work fine. There are many brands of pH down available.

Writing down the quantity of pH up or pH down that is added (for future reference) is a good method for putting together an identical solution in the future.

E. The electrodes should be rinsed in clean water before the meter is turned off.

pH Drift

The pH should be checked daily and adjusted if necessary because many fertilized solutions will drift significantly upward or downward in pH in less than 24 hours. Organic fertilizers tend to drift upward in pH after mixed, and may continue to do so a day or up to a few days after the solution is mixed. Adding molasses and avoiding certain fertilizers can keep the upward pH drift in a solution (organic or chemical-organic) to a minimum.

For fertilizer solutions with organic nutrients, pH drift is most common after the solution is mixed, and when certain nutrients in the reservoir run low.

Making an organic (or chemical-organic) solution a day or two in advance, with molasses (1.5ml per gallon of water) is a good starting point.

How to Use and Clean the pH Pen

If a pH pen is not cleaned after each day it is used, it can be hard to get accurate readings and it may not calibrate to the correct reading, especially if organic fertilizers are used. Using a cleaning solution before it is put away helps calibrate the pen accurately. The pen should be allowed to stay moist when it is put away. A few drops of calibrating solution in the bottom cap helps the electrodes stay moist. Cleaning the pH pen with clean tap water and a Q-tip works too, and saves money. When a Q-tip is used, it is recommended to gently pull the fluff away from the stick so that the soft cotton-batting can be moved between tough spaces. Care should always be taken with the glass, because it can break and start to give weird readings without a grower noticing the error.

After the pen is rinsed, pH buffer 7.0 solution is used to calibrate the pen. The meter should read 7.0. It may take several seconds to reach a stable reading. The pen can read 7.2 for a few seconds, and then it can slowly move down before it reads a constant 7.0.

A cheap bottle of pH 4.0 should be used once in a while to determine the condition of the pH meter in order to see that the pen calibrates at two different numbers, 4.0 and 7.0.

After the pH pen is calibrated, it should be rinsed well with clean water before taking a reading. The pen should be rinsed well with clean water after each reading. If the water is good, clean running cold tap water, the pen will often stay at one number when it is rinsed.

If the pH pen is really clean and calibrated properly, it should stay calibrated for several readings.

When the calibration does read differently it is probably because the pen needs a cleaning. If the meter is not clean and it is calibrated, all readings can be inaccurate. Weak batteries can also throw off the readings and make the pH pen function at a slower speed.

Hydroponic Mediums
Choosing a Hydroponic Medium
Choosing the proper hydroponic medium is the most important factor for a successful hydroponic garden. All mediums react to a fertilizing program different-

ly, and the cost of mediums varies dramatically. Some local materials (e.g. fir bark, wood chips, small stones, and coconut fibers) are available locally for a cheap price. Most large-scale hydroponic farms use large quantities of local materials to keep the costs down, but a hobbyist may get better yields from commercial products such as clay, rockwool, or sterilized soilless mix that is cheap and convenient for smaller gardens. For a hobbyist, purchasing a hydroponic medium (e.g. rockwool) from the local garden shop may be a cheaper (and better quality) solution than tracking down a free medium.

For any medium, it is safe to feed for 3 to 6 days, then flush for 1 day with plain. An option with flushing is to use plain water and 1 to 2ml of hydrogen peroxide to defend against pests in the root zone. A grower can flush throughout a plant's life cycle, until harvest is within two weeks. Two weeks prior to harvest, growers often flush out the medium with plain water, a clearing solution followed with plain water, or a low PPM solution (i.e. 0 to 400PPM) to get maximum flavor.

Preparing Mediums

Perlite compacts and should stand in a container of water for about a half hour. Fine particles of perlite will sink to the bottom of the water. The floating perlite is useful. The bottom of the barrel can go into compost or garden. Perlite is a good medium, but it does not cling onto elements. Therefore, plants must be well fed.

Clay floats, and should be soaked or sprayed until the water running through it becomes clear. Rinsing clay is similar to washing rice until the water runs clear. Clay is negatively charged and attracts positive ions such as calcium and potassium. Soaking rock-like mediums such as clay in water and 35% hydrogen peroxide (i.e. 2 to 5 ml per gallon of water) helps to sterilize the medium from any potential diseases. Sun heat helps sterilize mediums too.

Careful Alert: Perlite and other mediums can clog the feeding system and prevent the solution from pumping in or draining. All screens and filters may need a periodic cleaning and the pump should have panty hose (if used) cleaned during a reservoir change.

Reusing Mediums

All mediums (except disposable mediums like rockwool) can be reused if all roots are removed from the medium, and medium is sterilized between crops.

For example, clay, soilless mix, and round stones can be used indefinitely. Mediums can safely be sterilized with an application of 35% hydrogen peroxide (approximately 5 ml per gallon of water). Most mediums such as perlite can be composted or used immediately to improve soil. For example, broken down wood chips can go into compost, while perlite and soilless mix can go directly into the garden.

Mediums should be cleaned as soon as a crop is completed to avoid molds. Molds often build up while a moist medium (e.g. clay) sits unused. If necessary, a citrus cleanser can be used to clean medium so that all molds and waxy buildup are removed. After the citrus cleanser is applied, the medium should be rinsed with plain water to remove the soap-like bubbles. A little leftover cleanser in the medium will not harm the plants.

Reusing Soilless Mix
When the indoor or outdoor crop is finished, soilless mix can be sterilized with calcium peroxide so that the medium can be reused to grow more crops. This is beneficial, because after each crop is done, the grow mix retains its investment value, since it can be reused indefinitely. Only new fertilizers need to be added for each additional crop. Chemical fertilizers can be applied a little heavier in areas of adequate rainfall because the mix will get a natural flush.

Organically Grown
When organic fertilizers are used (or very little chemical ferilizers) the mix will retain its quality.

All organic nitrogen sources, such as blood meal, fish meal, feather meal, earthworm castings, chicken manure, and canola meal are effective only for a single outdoor growing season.

Phosphorous needs to be replenished each year. Bonemeal and rock phosphate work well independently or as a combination.

Mineral potash sources, such as greensand and crushed granite, extend their usefulness beyond a single season. The minerals will break down slowly over time, releasing potash to the roots. Fast-acting potash, good for a single season, is available in kelp meal and wood ashes.

Kelp meal also provides most of the necessary trace minerals for the plant, but should be added for each new crop.

Hydroponic Feeding Formulas
Buying a pH buffered fertilizer is the easiest way to feed properly!!!
For Vegetative Growth
Most hydroponic formulas are purchased in 1 to 3 parts. Using any commercial product's recommended rate works okay. The pH buffered fertilizers are most user friendly. Here are some basic formulas that work.

A. Calcium nitrate: 1.5 grams per liter (quart) or $1\frac{1}{2}$ teaspoons per gallon, dissolved in a small quantity of warm or hot water (1-liter) before adding to reservoir.

B. Potassium phosphate: $\frac{1}{3}$ gram per liter (quart) or $\frac{1}{4}$-teaspoon per gallon, dissolved in a small quantity ($\frac{1}{2}$ to 1-liter) of hot water.

C. Potassium sulphate: $\frac{1}{3}$ gram per liter (quart) or $\frac{1}{6}$-teaspoon per gallon, dissolved separately in warm or hot water.

D. Magnesium sulphate (Epsom salts): $\frac{1}{4}$ to $\frac{1}{2}$ gram per liter (quart) or $\frac{1}{4}$-teaspoon per gallon, dissolved in warm or hot water (1-liter).

E. Chelated trace elements: $\frac{1}{10}$-teaspoon per gallon or $\frac{1}{2}$-teaspoon per 5 gallons, dissolved separately in warm water. Kelp, or kelp and a mineral powder can be used in place of chelated trace elements.
     This solution mixture will be around 1,300PPM when read on a TDS meter. Solution should always fall between 1,000 and 1,500PPM, unless medium is being flushed with dilute solution (i.e. 800PPM) or with plain water (very briefly) to remove salts. The ph should be adjusted to fall between 6.0 to 6.6.

     Option: Seaweed products, humic acid, and vitamin B-1 may be added in small quantities. The PPM should be no higher than 1,500 if other products are added.

For Flowering Stage
Most hydroponic formulas are purchased in 1 to 3 parts. Using any commercial product's recommended rate works well. The pH buffered fertilizers are most user friendly. Here are some basic formulas that work.

A. Calcium nitrate: add 1.0 gram per liter (quart) or 1-teaspoon per gallon, dissolved separately in a small quantity of water (1-liter) before adding to reservoir. During late flowering, the calcium nitrate can be lowered to .5 to 1.0 gram per liter (quart).

B. Potassium phosphate: ⅔ gram per liter (quart) or ½-teaspoon per gallon, dissolved separately in a small quantity (i.e. ½-liter) of hot water.

C. Potassium sulphate: ⅕ to ¼ gram per liter (quart) dissolved separately in hot water.

D. Magnesium sulphate (Epsom salts): ¼ to ½ gram per liter (quart) or ¼-teaspoon per gallon, dissolved separately in hot water (1-liter).

E. Chelated trace elements: ⅒-teaspoon per gallon or ½-teaspoon per 5 gallons, dissolved separately in a small quantity of water (1-liter) before adding to reservoir. Kelp, or kelp and a mineral powder can be used in place of chelated trace elements.

This solution mixture will be around 1,300 when read on a TDS meter. The solution should always fall between 1,000 and 1,500PPM, unless medium is being flushed periodically with dilute solution(i.e. have the PPM drop to about 800PPM) or with plain water briefly to remove salts.

The pH should be adjusted to fall between 5.5 to 6.3.

Options: Seaweed products, humic acid, and vitamin B-1 may be added in small quantities.

Organic Hydroponics
The formulas in this section are designed for mediums that drain well such as perlite, coconut fibers, and clay pellets. These formulas will also work fine for soilless mixes such as Sunshine MIx® and Jiffy Mix™. These formulas have been formulated to give marijuana plants all the necessary primary and secondary elements, as well as the trace elements necessary for vigorous growth. No salts will accumulate with the organic ingredients, which will provide a fine tasting smoke. If quality is an issue and so is volume, the following sample formulas are definitely worth a try.

For complete control, cheap and light perlite is recommended for the medium because it does not alter the solution pH and fertilizers do not cling to it. Perlite also allows lots of air to get in the spaces when solution drains through it. However, perlite needs regular irrigation such as a few waterings a day or continuous irrigation. Not for the sake of food necessity, but for the fact that dry perlite sends out a dust. This dust can collect on the top of leaves.

Clay is good medium, but it is heavy and a little expensive. It is negatively charged and will hold some positive ions such as calcium and potassium. All mediums can be flushed with plain water regularly to remove salts.

Materials that alter the pH can be of use to keep the pH down, such as clay. Also, holding some water and nutrients can be good too, especially between feedings when the water is drained from the growing medium.

Vegetative Growth

Any recommended rate from an organic fertilizer manufacturer should work fine, but feeding needs to be more precise during bloom. If chemicals are used during vegetative growth, and organics are used during bloom, nobody will be able to tell the difference from a garden grown only with organics. This is a way to make tasty produce on a skinny budget.

Sample Formulas
Vegetative Growth Formula #1

Use the manufacturer's recommended rate for Sea Mix™ 3-2-2, or two-thirds of the recommended rate for Alaska Fish Fertilizer®, combined with the recommended rate for liquid kelp. In addition, pH up or pH down can be added until the pH is between 6.0 and 6.5.

Adding Epsom salts (magnesium sulphate), ½ to 1-teaspoon per 5 gallons will help combat magnesium and sulphur deficiencies.

Special note: all pH testing and addition of a pH up or pH down is optional, although recommended. Hydrogen peroxide usage at 1 to 3 ml per gallon is recommended to keep the medium clean.

Vegetative Growth Formula #2

When it comes time for the second feeding, the fertilizing can be repeated. Below is an optional solution to use:

Sea Mix™, two-thirds of the manufacturer's recommended rate; humic acid (made from organic molecules created from the breakdown of organic matter) at one-half to two-thirds of the recommended rate; pH up or pH down until the pH hits 6.0 to 6.5.

Vegetative Growth Improvisation Formulas #3

Since the pH of a water supply varies from town to town and city to city, it is possible to use different organic fertilizers to balance the pH. To lower the water's pH, one custom formula is to make a tea with worm castings and add fish emulsion or Earth Juice®. To raise pH in the water, going a little heavier on the wood ashes is an option. There are many other organic fertilizers with varying pH readings.

A tea of composted steer manure and liquid kelp can be good for a near-neutral water supply.

Every organic fertilizer will alter the pH of a solution to a different degree.

Flowering

A grower can apply any commercial fertilizer and mix it at the recommended rate. Results will be fine. But, in order to grow specific plants productively and with the lowest cost, making custom formulations is the way to go. All large-scale farms know the importance of making their own fertilizers, which is a major expense once the farm is set up.

During flowering, a grower cannot afford to be sloppy. Feeding is more critical and plants use more nutrients when they are producing flowers.

Sample Formulas
Bloom Formula #1

1. Four teaspoons per gallon of Earth Juice®Bloom.
2. Four teaspoons per gallon of Earth Juice®Grow.
3. Four teaspoons of bat guano per gallon. Guano should be placed into a teabag or added directly into the tank. Bat guano can cause stomach aches when it is used in a recirculating hydroponic system, even with minimal exposure. Using the replacement (potassium phosphate) from the chemical cheat sheet (below) is safer than bat guano. Organically, using more Greenfire®Earth Juice Bloom is another option.
4. Growth Plus (Nitrozyme®) at $\frac{1}{2}$-teaspoon per gallon.

Cannabis' diet during flowering differs from its diet during vegetative growth.

5. Epsom salts (magnesium sulphate) at .5 to 1 gram per quart (liter). Epsom salts should be dissolved in warm water before adding to nutrient solution.

6. One gram per gallon of sulphate of potash (potassium sulphate) or 2 grams per quart (liter) of wood ashes. Sulphate of potash should be mixed separately in hot water for it to completely dissolve.

7. Finally, pH is adjusted 5.5 to 6.5 with natural pH up or natural pH down.

Options

A grower can add the following to the above formula before adjusting pH.

1. Humic acid at 1-teaspoon per gallon or at ¼ to ⅓ the recommended rate.

2. For other trace minerals, a grower can add half to full recommended rate of liquid kelp.

3. Adding 1 tablespoon of molasses and two teaspoons of yeast into 1 quart

(liter) is a cheap homemade catalyst. The mixture should be dissolved before it is added to the tank. It will add enzymes and help to combat upward pH drift.

4. The solution should sit one or two nights so that pH stabilizes. Running a pump in the solution can help keep the solution agitated. Sometimes, some of the materials, such as bat guano, will flow to the bottom, but most of this formula will stay nicely mixed.

The pH of this solution will drift less upward, the longer it sits in the nutrient tank.

5. pH should be monitored daily and adjusted to 5.5 to 6.5, using either a natural pH up or a natural pH down. Adjusting the formula to a lower pH is a good way to deal with upward pH drift.

Chemical Cheat Sheet

Use .5 to 1 gram of calcium nitrate instead of Earth Juice®Grow and Earth Juice ®Bloom; use chelated trace minerals ($\frac{1}{2}$-teaspoon for every 5 gallons) while canceling the usage of Growth Plus™ (Nitrozyme®) and Pyro Clay™; use potassium phosphate at $\frac{1}{2}$ to $\frac{3}{4}$ gram per quart (liter) while eliminating the bat guano. The potassium levels can be changed during various stages of bloom to accommodate phosphorous levels.

Bloom Formula #2

1. Four grams per quart (liter) of Pure Earthworm castings. Worm castings can be wrapped in panty hose, a teabag, or cheesecloth. Squeezing the castings in the bag periodically helps to release the fertilizer more quickly.

2. Four teaspoons per gallon of Earth Juice®Bloom .

3. Four teaspoons of bat guano per gallon. Guano can be put in a teabag or panty hose. Guano should be squeezed periodically to release the fertilizer. Bat guano can cause stomachaches when it is used in a recirculating hydroponic system, even with minimal exposure. Using the replacement (potassium phosphate) from the chemical cheat sheet is safer than bat guano. Organically, using more Greenfire®Earth Juice Bloom (recommended rate) is another choice.

4. Growth Plus™ (Nitrozyme®) at 1-teaspoon per gallon.

5. Epsom salts (magnesium sulphate) at .5 to 1 gram per quart (liter). Epsom salts should be dissolved in warm water before adding them to a nutrient solution.

Using organic hydro formulas are simple with a garden this close to home.

6. One gram per gallon of sulphate of potash (Potassium Sulphate) or 2 grams per quart (liter) of wood ashes. Sulphate of potash should be mixed separately in hot water to completely dissolve the crystals before adding them to the nutrient solution.

7. The pH should be checked daily and adjusted to 5.5 to 6.5. A lower number is better for an upward drifting pH.

Options

1. Pyro Clay can be added at 1 gram per liter.

2. Humic acid can be added at 1-teaspoon per gallon or at ¼ to ⅓ the recommended rate.

3. For other trace minerals, half to full recommended rate of liquid kelp may be added.

4. Adding 1 tablespoon of molasses and 2 teaspoons of yeast into 1 quart (liter) works as a catalyst. The mixture should be dissolved before it is added to the tank. The mixture will add enzymes and help combat upward pH drift.

Chemical Cheat Sheet

Use .5 to 1 gram of calcium nitrate instead of Earth Juice®Grow and Earth Juice ®Bloom; use chelated trace minerals (½-teaspoon for every 5 gallons) while canceling the usage of Growth Plus™ (Nitrozyme®) and Pyro Clay™; use potassium phosphate at ½ to ¾ gram per quart (liter) while eliminating the bat guano. The potassium levels can be changed during various stages of bloom to accommodate phosphorous levels.

Special Notes (for All Organic Hydroponic Formulas)

Solution should be topped up regularly (i.e. daily to weekly) with plain water or nutrient solution, depending on how the pH, PPM, and water level changes.

The pH of the solution should be checked and modified after adding liquid to reservoir. Drawing a top-up line in the reservoir with a permanent felt-tip pen helps to make topping-up the reservoir a brainless exercise. Large reservoirs that can run a few days to a week with proper pH and PPM make things even more brainless.

These organic formulas on pages 97 to 101 should be somewhere near 1,500PPM when read on a TDS meter after they are mixed, if the water supply reads at 0PPM. A PPM meter can be used as a reference meter. A grower should take readings once in a while and see if the PPM goes up or down.

If the PPM stays the same or goes down just slightly, adding the regular mixed solution to the reservoir should suffice.

Making a solution that keeps a constant PPM (or slightly lowering PPM) gives the plant the exact elements they need until the reservoir becomes empty and is pH buffered: this is the path to feeding perfection. With this method, the reservoir is easy to clean before adding new solution. This is efficient gardening.

If the PPM goes up, more water should be added to the tank to dilute the solution. With this approach, complete changes of solution are recommended, especially for larger plants that use up more nutrient than water.

After a couple of weeks, an organic hydroponic solution can bring on odors, depending on the fertilizer (e.g. stinky bat guano).

If a PPM meter is used in an organic or chemical-organic garden, what works is changing the solution when the PPM drops to ⅓ to ½ of the original strength (i.e. PPM drops from 1,500 to 500 to 750PPM). The waste can be poured out anywhere in an outdoor garden. Or, addition of the same formula can be added from time to time to replenish nutrients, if there is no smell. Or, for the trained eye, individual nutrients can be added such as Earth Juice® Grow, bat guano, etc., as deficiencies are spotted.

Nitrogen consumption is probably the heaviest from all the elements in the formulations. Changing the solution and replenishing all nutrients is the best move to keep things simple.

Optional: Foliar Feeding

Note: All pH testing and addition of pH up is optional. The results will still be beneficial if the wetting agent is left out of the recipe.

Foliar feeding should be stopped 2 to 3 weeks prior to harvest so that all residues are rinsed off, and so that nutrients have time to be flushed out of the plant tissue. Flushing allows for top quality. To protect the lungs, a respirator should be worn while foliar feeding.

Formula A

1. $\frac{1}{3}$-teaspoon or 3ml of Nitrozyme®(Growth Plus™) per quart (liter) of water, or any liquid kelp used at recommended rate for foliar feeding.

2. $\frac{1}{16}$-teaspoon or .25ml vitamin B_1 per quart (liter) of water.

3. Organic wetting agent (manufacturer's recommended rate).

4. Optional: pH up or pH down (to bring the pH to 6 to 6.5 after adding the above ingredients).

4

Maintaining an Outdoor Garden

Introduction

The following important variables will be discussed in this chapter in detail:

A. Light quality (i.e. lots of sunshine). In general, more light is better, but some breeds can grow well in lower light levels. Also, pruning and bending plants can bring more usable light to the plant. Smart outdoor growers design their gardens so that they can maximize sunlight hours for the entire growing season.

B. The right plant. The strain will make or break a crop. With all other variables perfect, a grower can produce a failed garden if the plant is not suited for the climate, or if it is unproductive. Certain strains may prove more resistant to problems that are beyond the grower's control such as frost, excessive rainfall, fluctuating root temperatures, hailstorms, heavy winds, or inadequate nutrients.

C. Proper feeding and watering. A good medium is necessary for the plants to reach their full potential. The plants' diet will affect yield and quality. Underwatering plants can be bad news.

D. Ideal root temperature. If the root temperature is good, plant growth can be maximized. Plant roots that are under the ground can be cooled or heated, depending upon the climate where the plants are grown.

The plants in front look like hell. This is crop failure and could stem from a multitude of problems.

E. Ideal air temperature. These factors are beyond a grower's control if he grows under the sun, but they can be controlled in a greenhouse. A grower should use the most productive calendar months for growing.

F. Predator control. A grower must do his homework here, or he could end up with no plants at any given time.

G. Care. Plants grow better if they are loved, rather than just stared at with dollar signs in the eyes.

H. The proper gardening system. It is critical to use a system that leads to maximum productivity, with minimal waste. It is also critical to use a system that caters to particular needs. For example, does a grower want a low maintenance garden, or a more elaborate system that requires more effort in order to get the maximum yield in the minimum amount of time? This chapter gives all the details a grower may want to know in order to build a custom gardening system that will fulfill particular needs, such as soilless mix gardens, and hydroponic systems that use more complicated irrigation techniques. Soilless mix is the easiest and most forgiving medium for both the novice and pro.

Transplanting

Plants can be transplanted at any time of the vegetative growth phase. As a general rule, plants should be able to spread their roots and not become too rootbound. Plants should not be transplanted during budding.

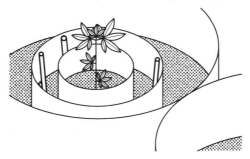

Transplanted with predator protection.

Transplanting is easy; here are the steps:

A. A hole is made.

B. Plant roots are placed into the hole. Roots should not be exposed!

C. The roots are covered without being damaged.

D. Roots are moistened if medium is dry.

Plants can be transplanted from one medium to another. For example, plants in rockwool, clay, perlite, soilless mix, or dirt can go into any other medium.

Plant roots will adapt to various root environments. The key is to feed the roots properly at all times. For example, a plant in peat moss or soilless mix that is transplanted to clay or perlite will need a new feeding program, because soilless mix can be constantly irrigated or it can go days between irrigation. However, roots located in a medium such as clay cannot go days between waterings, given that plants are grown under a strong climate. The same holds true if a plant is transplanted from a medium like rockwool or clay into soil or soilless mix.

Plants should never be transplanted during budding because the plants can receive too much of a shock.

All predator control—such as protection from rats, slugs, and bears—should be in place when plants are transplanted.

Water Supply
Pure and Not So Pure
Using pure, clean water is the easiest way to increase the yield in the garden.

The quality of an outdoor water supply will vary from creek to creek, river to river, spring to spring, pond to pond, various artesian well sources, rainwater zones, and so on. For example, a company may have sprayed toxic substances to kill vegetation nearby. The residue may have a long, full life and therefore toxify the surrounding water supplies.

Nevertheless, getting water from a creek or other water source that runs through chemically untreated land would be just fine.

Purifying Water
Water filters, reverse osmosis machines, distillation devices, and rainwater reservoirs are all methods of obtaining pure water.

All of the above purifying methods can be performed for large and small quantities of water. Machines and filters to handle larger amounts of water will cost more.

Some machines and filters remove dissolved solids better than others. The better units normally cost more.

Removing Chlorine Only
There are cheap filters that can be attached to faucets that remove chlorine from the water. Often, chlorine is the domestic gardener's worst enemy.

Desalinization: Diluted Sea Water
Desalinizing sea water is an expensive option for making quality use of sea water, although prices of these units have come down significantly over the past few years.

Water should be a few miles from a flat creek or river that runs into an ocean, for salt water travels upstream. Watering with diluted sea water will retard the growth rate. The rate will vary depending on the saline content in the water.

Water Temperature
Preferably the water will have a temperature near 65 to 70°F. However, watering with a temperature between 60 and 80°F is also okay.

Any running water will work. If cold water is used, it is recommended to use a system that needs infrequent irrigation, or a slow drip so that the roots do not get constantly saturated with chilly water.

Adaptability to water temperature varies from strain to strain.

Sunshine
Without this big ball in the sky, outdoor cultivation would be impossible. To some, the sun is easily overlooked as a cultivation tool, while for others it is an important static growing device that one plays with to maximize yields, lower watering needs, and alter the timing of harvest. The following information is a more detailed look at these examples.

Marijuana plants love to get as much sun as possible. Anyone who has grown indoors and has played with light intensity will see this. But the more sun a plant receives, the more water it will need.

If water supply is not an issue, then full sun is the way to go. Plants will mature sooner with larger buds in full sun. However, the buds may get so dense and large that additional support for them is a must.

If water is lacking at the site, whether from inadequate water because of hot weather or from neglect, it can be detrimental to the plant's life and productivity. An option here is to plant in a spot where trees or other obstacles

Southern and southwest slopes receive plenty of sunlight.

block out a certain percentage of sunlight; for example, in a location where plants receive only 8 hours of direct light on the longest day of the year.

When blocking aids such as trees are used, it is possible to manipulate the blockage for certain times of day. For example, a set of trees can block out the morning, evening, or afternoon sun. It is best not to leave out afternoon sun. The less direct light a plant gets, the longer it will take to be ready for harvesting.

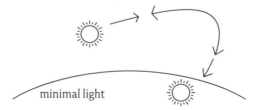
minimal light

South and southwest mountain slopes and flat lands receive lots of sunshine.

Steady Harvesting with One Strain

Growing with identical clones or different seedlots offers an opportunity to stagger the harvest. For example, a strain fully matures in early September when grown in full sun. If identical clones are taken and planted in different

Top: The flower forced buds are ready for the picking. Middle: Plants are covered daily to induce flowering with a shorter photoperiod. Bottom: Plants during early flower in their flower-forcing zone.

amounts of sunshine, the ripening time can be extended throughout the fall. If double harvests are included in the program by removing the larger tops soon before maturity, then the harvest season can be extended further.

These techniques are really efficient and effective for a smaller grower who has the time to try to get the largest possible harvest and yet have steady work. Another option (and depending on the situation, maybe the best option) and the quickest harvesting technique is to pull all the plants at once. Some people like harvest season, while others like to get it over with.

The time of transplanting from the indoor environment may affect the timing of harvest. For example, one fresh cutting transplanted on May 15 may finish at the same time as its genetic twin sister transplanted on June 1, given that they were exposed to the same sunlight conditions. However, two identical clones of another strain may finish budding at different times, given that they were also transplanted on May 15 and June 1. In the second case, both clones received the same hours of sunshine.

Flower Forcing

Marijuana plants in vegetative growth can be triggered to flower if the plants are given a daily photoperiod that is less than 12 hours. For example, plants can be forced to flower if they are exposed to complete darkness in a greenhouse for 12 hours (or slightly more) per day.

Temperature

Air Temperature

Plants can grow and adapt to all sorts of climates. This means that what is good for one plant of the same species is not necessarily good for another. Since most gardeners are after quality and quantity, they often grow breeds that are area specific. Plants can flower above 90 to 100°F and do wonders. Some plants prefer warm days and cool nights. Some plants prefer warm days and warm nights. Some plants can do well in various conditions, while others cannot.

To play it safe, marijuana plants should be grown during frost-free conditions, since spring and fall frosts have the potential to screw up (or kill) the plant. All other factors, such as excessive rainfall, poor light, high heat, cool temperatures, etc., can be dealt with as long as the strain is acclimatized to the local weather conditions, and the plants are well fed.

Root Temperature

Root temperature should not be too cool nor too hot. A temperature near 65 to 70°F is recommended. However, root temperature that falls between 60 to 80°F is sufficient. Different plant strains have varying levels of adaptability to the root temperature factor.

Plants that have their roots underground can be kept cooler in hot climates and warmer in cool climates.

Pruning and Bending

Pruning is a process of pinching the top shoot(s) so the plant will grow bushier and provide more tops, while staying shorter. Pruning is recommended if the vegetative cycle is long enough for the hormones to effectively transfer to the new set of tops (at least one month of vegetative growth after pruning is recommended). The plant hormones in the plant's top shoot are auxins, which cause a plant to grow tall. Auxins travel to the next set of top shoots after the original top shoot is removed. With pruning, auxins will form in several shoots to promote several leaders of new growth.

Pruning a month before budding or even earlier (anywhere from two months after germination) will result in more tops. These tops may be nearly identical in size and should be close in size to that of the top had it not been pruned. Pruning may be done more than once during the vegetation process, thus creating a bud-multiplying effect. Some strains accept pruning and grow large buds, while some strains will have downsized bud production as a result of pruning. Once again, it is good to have an affiliation with and a history of desired strains, so that production is maximized with pruning methods.

Predator Pruning

At some time during cultivating practices, a predator such as a slug may be chowing down anywhere its taste buds desire. The plant can recover if enough vegetation is left and it is not just a stick. This will depend on the plant's rate of production and the amount of vegetation being eaten by the predator.

In the early seedling, late seedling, and early vegetation phases, a slug will eat the plant down to a stick and not leave any green vegetation. A deer, on the other hand, may nibble on new growing shoots or on the entire plant, and then walk away. A plant lives through this treatment, or it doesn't. If it does, every shoot that

The bottom leaves, which get very little light, are being pruned from this plant.

was eaten will result in the plant growing differently than it would normally.

One source revealed that his best plant in a four-plant plot was the result of a slug pruning job. Therefore, slug damage may not be detrimental.

A similar problem is broken limb damage from an animal such as a bear walking over a plant in its path. Sometimes the broken limb can be taped with duct tape and it will be fine, but sometimes the break will cause wilting and death to the branch.

This lower branch is trained from the ground.

Bending

Bending is a process of physically moving a limb, branch, or main stock to a new position. There are many ways of doing this. A piece of string or twine may be tied in a knot around the limb and then tied to another string, a log, a tree, or a nearby stake.

Bending allows shoots that have been deprived of light to receive intense light. The exposed shoots can now put on mass much more quickly than when exposed to low light levels, which causes slow and unproductive growth.

The stake in the grow bag gives the plant support.

Bending is done to obtain maximum light for the inner vegetation and to ensure that all vegetation receives more light. Bending is a good idea indoors or out, but the limbs should not be bent too hard or beyond a point they can't take physically. This will take practice. Yields will always increase.

If a limb breaks, a grower should immediately look at the vegetation along the broken limb to see if it looks normal. If it is not wilted, then string or tape can be used to secure the break. The limb may also need careful staking. If the limb is severely wilted, cutting it off carefully will permit the plant to heal itself.

Limbs of the plants in this beautiful garden are supported with string tied to stakes.

Bending can also be used to support limbs and stalks in the event the buds become so large that the plant cannot support them on its own. Sometimes a happy medium is reached when the buds become heavy and the limbs adopt a more horizontal position. This naturally exposes the inner leaves to more light and allows more photosynthesis to take place.

This organized garden has stakes in place well before they are needed.

Predators

Many aspects of cultivation are universal, but predators aren't. For example, a predator that hangs out and lives on a semi-elevated southwest slope may not live on the northern slope or the other side of the valley. (For example, a rodent could be attracted to that sunny spot and to the vegetation there.) The best way to deal with potential damage from living organisms is by keeping accurate records of the problems encountered.

Deer

Deer seem to be put off by mothballs (scattered around the plot every month or two), and tall fencing. Misting plants with plain water and tossing on fine-blended bonemeal or bat guano immediately afterward has been reported to do wonders. Also, goats can be a problem because they will devour all buds and leaves in sight.

Bugs

Bugs don't seem to be a problem if the growing medium and growing conditions are at a decent standard. A little prevention can involve planting a few cloves of garlic at the transplanting time and weekly foliar feeding of liquid

Not all visitors are harmful.

kelp (i.e. Nitrozyme® (Growth Plus™) or another brand) from the time the plants are young through near maturity.

To deal with a bug problem immediately, it is recommended to apply an organic insecticidal soap combined with Nitrozyme® (Growth Plus™) every 4 to 10 days while wearing a respirator. Rubbing the bottoms of the leaves gently while spraying will help to ensure that all of the areas get covered and some bugs get squished. The war psychology of bug-smearing may be argued among scientists and other interest groups.

Spider mites seem to be the rookie's most undetected predator, next to the rat. Spider mites are bugs that suck fluids from the plants, and they can spread diseases. The plants then spend time dealing with the stress, which affects yield. Understanding what makes mites thrive is half the battle. They like a hot, dry room with weak plants. They are discouraged by high humidity, and they incubate at a highly productive rate when the temperature rises above 80°F. Misting adds humidity, which helps the stomata to open. This is particularly helpful during foliar feeding, to increase the nutrient intake. Stroking the plants stimulates hormonal activity that will increase growth.

Daily mists are okay until plants are about 3 weeks into the budding process, after which a twice-a-week misting is recommended. Misting is reduced during flowering because the buds may begin to mold with over-misting. This will occur in mold-sensitive strains or in plants that are not as healthy as they should be.

There is no cut-and-dried method for determining exactly when to stop misting, but problems from too much misting are more likely to occur when buds have been formed for 3 weeks or more.

Spraying the undersides of the leaves well is the key, because that is where the spider mites hang. Nevertheless, if spider mites become a problem, spraying every 4 to 7 days with an organic insecticidal soap combined with ½-teaspoon per quart of Nitrozyme® (Growth Plus™) will help. The combination of the two is more effective than straight soap. It is advised to rinse the plants the day after the soap spray is applied, using plain water. A respirator should be worn whenever fertilizers or insecticides are sprayed in order to keep the mist out of the lungs.

If spider mites cannot be dealt with at this level, regular misting and foliar feeding with liquid kelp should be enough of a preventative tactic to ensure the mite population does not get out of hand, unless plants are weak from poor cultivating methods.

Predator mites are an expensive method for dealing with the problem. If predator mites are used, it is still a good idea to lower the spider mite population with insecticides before introducing the spider mites. However, it is recommended to wait a few days for the chemical ingredients of the insecticide to wear off before the introduction of the predator mites so that they won't get zapped.

When mites are at a tolerable level, all else must be going okay. The more mite-free your plants, the better. A grower should not be over-stressed because of a few mites.

The mite population should be as minimal as possible on the mother plant(s). When a mother plant gets a disease, new clones may be hard to root. They may still be productive, but the disease will be a hindrance and can interrupt the normal schedule.

Misting plants daily or every second day soon before or right after the lights come on also helps keep other bugs, such as thrips, under control. Applying an organic insecticidal soap at the rate of ½-teaspoon per quart of water, or as recommended on the package, also works in a crisis. The soap should be rinsed off a couple of days after spraying to remove the soap film from the plants' stomatas. Stomatas are vital for transpiration. One organic method for keeping bugs under control is planting garlic in soil or soilless mix. Another organic method to kill bugs is to use pyrethrins, which is an extract from the chrysanthemum plant. A health conscious grower probably would not want to get near the pyrethrins, organic or not.

Other methods to kill all bugs are to use malathion, diazinon, etc. These materials have rather short half-lives, but again they stink like serious toxicity and should not have a place in the garden, except as a last resort.

Anybody needing to use a bug spray, should polish up on his horticulture skills and grow healthy plants, rather than rely on a toxic Band-Aid solution.

Slugs

A single to double layer of several-inch-high slug tape placed at various diameters around the stalks works well. Setting open containers of beer into the soil around the plot (covered so water can't dilute the beer) also works well. Raised containers or beds that are isolated and high off the ground seem to attract fewer slugs than spots on the ground's surface. Copper surrounding the plot supposedly works well, but it is expensive.

Using slug bait and slug tape is about 100% effective.

If the crop is in a life-or-death situation, it is environmentally friendlier to place the bait in plastic cups sloping downward at the outskirts of the plot, rather than to leave it exposed to the rain. In this way the slugs go in and eat and are then poisoned. Some make it back out, some won't.

The stuff must stay dry as long as possible because a little goes a long way, and handling less is always best. Reapplying a little Slug Death in the cups every 3 to 5 weeks is recommended to beat the nasty slug.

Small slugs can be hard to find and may leave holes all over the plant, which causes weakening of the plant tissue, which results in slower growth. Rubbing the leaves may be necessary to find these slimy critters.

Slugs are mainly spring feeders. They do their most damage in cool and wet spring conditions. Slugs and rain go hand in hand. They slow down in their movement and diet habits in the hot summer days.

Rats and Mice

Mice tend to like young seedlings, even those that have just germinated. However, once seedlings are 2 to 3 weeks old, mice tend to leave them alone. The seedling zone should be well sealed so that is 100% mouse proof, because they have been known to devour complete starter rooms. Utrasound® is a unit that sends out a frequency that deters mice and rats, yet is not heard by pets and family.

Rats, on the other hand, can be life-threatening to plants. Rats will eat a circle around the outer stalk, at the base of the plant. This will look similar to a tree that is being cut down by a lumberjack.

This removal of the plant tissue will cut off the flow of vital fluids from traveling up and down the plant. Plants will wilt and die soon afterward.

However, some plants can be saved, if they still look normal and healthy. To remedy the situation, it is recommended to cut out a piece of outer bark from a plant of the same species.

Then the patch should be placed over the bark that was eaten so that it connects to the upper and lower parts of the stalk, where the rat had stopped eating.

Now just a little Vaseline and tape will secure this patchwork. This patch will act like a suspension bridge so that it is possible to pass necessary components from the lower and upper sides of the stalk.

The new material will eventually be welded in place. The plant will be fine.

Mothballs around a plot may also act as a deterrent.

Rats do like eating some organic fertilizers such as canola meal and Flower Power.

Bears

Bears don't seem to cause problems unless they decide to give a garbage can or bag a closer inspection. After realizing that it is a lame food source, they tend to move on. Burying garbage bags and cans, and building a raised bed around their contained mix, will offer superior plant protection. Odds seem greater of no attack than of an attack to the plants.

Bears are most destructive in the early spring after a long winter nap, when floral and berry vegetation is low.

Rabbits
A fence (1 to 2 feet high) should be built around the plants in order to keep them out.

Mold
It is always best to prevent mold in the bud and stems by having an acclimatized strain that is known to handle the elements, and by regular foliar feeding with Nitrozyme® (Growth Plus™) or a quality liquid kelp. However, for whatever reason, a mold problem may occur. For mold problems, it is recommended to spray an organic fungicide with Nitrozyme® (Growth Plus™). There are other fungicides that are commonly available, such as organic fungicides and Wilson's® Bordeaux.

Disease
A strong strain and a good grow medium are needed at the preventative level. When a disease hits clones, starting again from seed may be the answer. Most diseases can be dealt with, unless the plant receives poor care.

Fusarium
When plants wilt not for lack of water, fusarium is a major possibility. Fusarium targets a plant with weak roots and a water temperature over 70°F. Roots often become unhealthy (brownish) in stagnant, warm water.

Keeping roots healthy (whitish) and water temperature below 70°F is the best preventative measure to deal with fusarium.

If fusarium hits a plant and it becomes wilted and sickly looking, the plant should be pulled immediately so that it will not hinder the other plants. If other plants share the same water (i.e. hydroponic gardening), hydrogen peroxide should be added to the water at a rate of 2 to 5ml per gallon to help sterilize the water.

5

Harvesting, Drying and Storing

The plants should be picked when they are ripe.

Often, females have pistils that change color at maturity, and the buds peak into a beautiful, natural, ornamental bud. Sometimes pistils will go from white (or a color) to a dead brown. The peak harvest time is often somewhere in between. However, other times the buds will overmature with a significant amount of healthy-looking pistils in the buds.

When some marijuana plants overmature, the buds will fluff-out, or become dry and old looking. The fine line in between full maturity and over aging is often the time to pick the buds since they are at their largest size with maximum beauty. Exact timing to pick will vary from plant to plant. Some overmature in style and still make a wonderful flower, while some will weaken so quickly that the grade is significantly decreased.

Picking

Outdoor growing creates many more variables than indoor growing. For example, a plant that isn't mold resistant may be plagued by mold before it is quite ripe. By the time it ripens, there may be no buds left to save. Therefore, calculated decision-making enters into the program.

Yet another situation is when a strain isn't quite finished before the frosts arrive. In this case, it is recommended to monitor such a plant and pick it when it looks like it can't go any further, or when mold seems to be lurking. All plants should be picked either in the morning or evening / night.

Top: The stalk is the waste product. These burn easy and quickly. Bottom left: Buds were picked and hung up by the stalks. Bottom right: Picking with shears.

Drying Buds

Indoors

Mature marijuana plants can be dried in locations such as a room (65 to 70°F) with a humidity of 30 to 50%. Some types can be dried in a solar dehydrator.

Marijuana plants can be hung to dry, or picked as they dry. Hanging buds to dry

Top: Removing the leaves is a tedious chore. Bottom left: Hanging the plant to dry emits the least amount of odor of any drying process. Bottom right: The dried buds are given a final manicure.

before picking is recommended for those that want to keep down the irritating odor of handled buds. Strains that grow odor-free will still release an odor when handled, especially when they are not dry. Picking all buds requires removing the larger leaves in the buds, then shaving the leaf near the bud with scissors or shears.

Buds dry more quickly when air is moved around via an oscillating fan, even when the humidity is a little high and the temperature is cool.

Dehumidifiers dramatically speed up the drying process.

Sweating buds after they initially dry can help pull moisture out of the stalks and into the leaf parts. Sweating can be done once, or more than once. Sweating for 1 day to several weeks is an option. Buds stored with a little moisture will be better than buds that are stored bone-dry, given all things equal. However, buds stored with too much moisture for too long can turn brown, which can lead to mold and / or rot. The line is not fine between mold and brown. However, the odor of the buds will change dramatically when mold sets in. When mold sets in, a musty smell will be obvious.

Outdoors

Some marijuana growers like to dry their crop in the bush, especially a forager that collects other wild, flowering plants, or, a homesteader that lives in the bush. There are a few basic options here: propane heat, wood heat, solar dehydrator, or electric heat with power drawn from a generator.

Propane heat is not recommended because it adds moisture and may make the job tough if the humidity cannot be dealt with. However, a canvas tent, which will absorb plenty of moisture, can allow the job to be done if there are no better options. In fact, drying buds is possible in a canvas tent when the doors are left open, even in rain when the humidity is high, but the color may be a little on the brown side.

Gas generators that provide electricity can give power for electric heaters and instruments such as dehumidifiers. However, generators are fairly bulky to move, and they need fuel—not the best option unless the setup is hassle free.

Solar dehydrators can utilize the energy of the sun to dry buds. This is a cost-effective device. They can be purchased at stores, or they can be homemade.

Wood heat is best used in a canvas wall tent, a plastic shack house, or a wood cabin. Wall tents are designed to use wood stoves, they keep a reasonable climate, and they are nice and portable, too.

If a wall tent is used, it should be set up near a decent supply of wood.

Many foragers who collect natural flowers to sell to wholesalers use portable drying methods.

The bottom line: the drying process is the wrong place to skimp.

Shake

Hash bags can be used to get some hash out of shake. Two books, *Hashish* by R. Clarke, and *Marijuana Gold: Trash to Stash* by Ed Rosenthal explain how to make use of lower-grade leaf and trimmings.

The waste leaf can be used for cooking, using 1 to 3oz of crushed leaf and trimmings for each pound of butter or oil. Baker's chocolate chips packaging has a good cookie recipe that uses 1 cup of butter. Butter is simmered with crushed leaf for a few minutes, then it should be strained. About 1 cup is left over.

Canning and Storing Dried Goods

Buds can be canned and stored in mason jars. They can be stored in plastic too, but plastic releases an odor.

Before storage, the jars should be washed with soap and water. Then they should be rinsed with clean water.

The next step is to boil the jars in water for 5 minutes before they are allowed to dry.

The jars should be delicately filled with the dry buds. The weight of the buds will not change if the buds are properly dried.

The mason jar lids should be placed in a saucepan and boiled for 3 to 5 minutes. Both sides of the lids should be dried with a cloth, then the lids should be immediately placed on the jars and the bands screwed on.

The jars should be left in a cool or cold spot for a night or two.

If the lids are secured properly, the lids will be popped down, not popped up. If they are popped up, pressing each lid down with sharp, quick taps can secure the lid with a downward placement.

Finally, the jars should be stored in a cool, safe spot. The shelf life is indefinite for flowers that have been properly dried.

6

Breeding

This book has emphasized the use of the right strain for particular growing conditions. Now we will look at many important factors a grower may want to know when breeding.

Breeding Decision Factors

Viable pollen (from sacks) of a male plant must contact the pistils from a female plant in order to produce seeds. The pistils of a female plant are located in the buds and at the nodes. Seeds can be made at any time the pistils are healthy, if the weather permits.

To determine which plants to breed, the breeder should pay attention to how successfully all the plants grow in the vegetative, early-flowering, and late-flowering states.

Types of Strains: Sativa versus Indica

Most plants grown these days are pure Sativa, pure Indica, or a sativa / indica cross.

Sativa

Sativa strains tend to have small clusters of buds that extend along the branches. The buds tend to have larger spaces between the clusters than Indica strains. Often, these plants grow to a tall height. The effects of smoking these plants is an upper high that tends to maintain an even high for a given time period before coming down. It is not a sharp up and down.

Even tiny buds can be pollinated for seeds.

In many cases, the user's mental attitude, tolerance, and physical fitness level will play a part in the high.

Indica

Indica strains normally grow to be small, bushy plants with dense buds at the tops and ends of the branches. Indica strains tend to have a heavy high that can be a bit of a downer. The high can be depressing or positive, depending on an individual's reaction to the drug. In many cases, the mental attitude, tolerance, and physical fitness level of the user will play a part in the high. For example, a person who feels very comfortable at home could feel very paranoid and uneasy in an unfamiliar, undesirable setting.

Indica / Sativa Crosses

These plants will look somewhere in between a pure Indica and a pure Sativa.

Physical Factors

Good breeding insight allows for the maintenance of desired traits, such as heavy-volume, fast maturation, good or bad odor, and a will to survive in a particular climate.

There are also fancy and advanced quality traits, such as pistil color, leaf pattern, bud density, and aroma during burning, but to make breeding simple, these specific traits have been left out of this discussion in favor of taking a common sense approach.

Plant Volume

Monitoring stalk diameter at the base of a plant and observing root mass will help in determining a larger volume plant. In general, larger-stalked plants are harder to pull out of the ground, which indicates a more elaborate root system. The root environment must be consistent for correctly determining root mass, because a highly oxygenated, well-fertilized root medium will allow a plant to make a more substantial root system in less space.

If small plants are preferred so that a garden needs less care, then a grower should look for small diameter stalks and less root mass. Plants with smaller stalks and less root mass will use a smaller amount of water and are not so prone to being blown over by heavy winds.

In order for a grower to accurately assess stalk and root mass, plants should be exposed to identical growing mediums and all other variables such as growing settings from germination throughout harvest.

A final test in determining volume is to calculate the yield at the harvest.

Fast / Late Maturation

Choosing plants that mature quickly will allow those timing traits to be passed on to the next generation, especially if the male and female are fast-maturing. Any inconsistencies will show up in the next generation if late and early-maturing plants are crossed. The crossed hybrids will have varying maturing times. However, some outdoor plants often have a sense as to when it is best to mature. A crop can always be a little late or a little early depending on the environmental conditions of the season.

Late plants may be desired, in order to capitalize on a long growing season. The amount of nitrogen used during budding can alter the harvest date.

This bud looks dry and a little fluffy, which is often a sign of not being hardy enough for the territory.

Nitrogen usage during budding will extend budding, but it can increase the yield if it is used to combat a nitrogen deficiency if it is not applied in excess.

Odor

Some plants will smell when they are young seedlings, some will not smell from seedlings throughout full maturity. Breeding plants that don't smell allows this trait to be passed on.

Potency

THC and other chemicals are responsible for the potency. Fortunately, looking for the crystal content on the buds explains this factor. In general, more crystals mean more potency. When buds have lots of crystals, they are potent. Many commercial seed strains give the thc percentage.

Environmental Factors

Plants that are growing in the particular climate in which they belong will look

This sorry sight is not where it's at.

green, strong, and have no holes in their leaves from disease, bugs, etc. Strong plants will also adjust to and grow well in the various local weather and root conditions.

Importance of Grow Medium

Not only is the climate important in determining the ideal strain, but so is the medium below. A strain grown in a soil mixture may do well in various hydroponic systems, or it may not. Some strains need more air down there than others, some more water, some more food and / or a slightly different diet. If hard work is performed on one cultivation technique, it is possible to

This plant is producing well under the local sky.

eventually find plants that make perfect matches to various environmental conditions.

Many commercial seed companies have descriptions and pictures about various strains so that a grower can find a suitable strain for his particular growing climate.

Elevation

Plants respond and adapt to the air at different elevations. It is more often easier to take a high-elevation plant and introduce it to a lower elevation than vice versa.

Light Levels

Plants can adapt to and utilize adverse weather to put on significant mass. Rainforest breeders have strains that grow in the cold and wet, while plants from another territory will turn pale and grow more slowly in the same adverse climate.

Continuous breeding—inbreeding and outbreeding (unrelated cross)—can give rise to strongly acclimatized plants.

It is easier to take a plant from adverse conditions and introduce it to a warmer, less adverse climate, than to take a plant from a warm, safe environment and throw it into a rainforest jungle.

Taking plants that grow well in low-light conditions can allow an outdoor grower to get a good yields in areas of good and poor sunlight.

Also, breeding low-light plants with other plants can pass on these characteristics to the next generation. Looking at the spaces between the nodes helps in determining how well some plants use light. Less space between the nodes is preferred.

Disease Resistance

Root diseases, such as leaf-spot fungus, exist in various soil conditions. Some plants can fight and live with the disease more easily than others.

Frost Resistance

Different plants can handle varying levels of frost. In the early spring, some plants can handle strong frosts, while others die or become mutated. In the fall, some plants can live through frosts of varying degree, while some plants will shut down, deteriorate, and mold in a light frost.

Drought Resistance

Some plants use more water than others and their leaves, stalks, and bud mass can be inferior to a plant grown alongside in identical conditions.

Mold Resistance

Some plants can put on significant rot-free mass in cold, rainy weather, while other plants will rot under identical growing conditions. Rainforest breeders know that without mold resistance in the plants, one is playing with fire in a climate zone that gets about 3.5 meters (more than 11 feet) of annual rainfall.

This crystal-coated bud shows no signs of disease in the leaves, such as holes or rust marks.

Breeding Tips

Seedlings can run in all sorts of types. They can be hybrids with scattered genetics, or purer strains with known characteristics. Good breeders generally have good seeds. An advantage of seedlings is that it is possible to grow different marijuana strains in the garden from a batch of seeds, although some seeds may be completely unproductive.

Easy Breed

The easiest way to produce outdoor seed in its natural setting is to leave a few plants in a clump. If all seedlings are from mother(s) that worked out well the year before, most new seeds should do fine the following year. Odds are that with four or more plants, males and females will show up to allow for reproduction. This method seems to work well for those who grow only outdoors from spring through harvest and then shut down. However, plants in all shapes and sizes may result if specific plants are not picked out for the breeding stock. Through continual inbreeding, the seed will eventually seem relatively uniform with regard to size, volume, maturation date, odor, and potency.

However, breeding the choice plants from seed that is continually inbred is recommended.

Making a Purebreed

A grower may want a pure strain so that he can produce a productive garden on demand using unknown seeds.

For starters, a grower should get two seedlots that are from different origins and grow the desired plants.

Then, the different seedlots should be crossed to make an F1 generation.

Now, inbreeding two plants from the F1 generation seedlot will produce an F2 generation.

Inbreeding two plants from an F2 generation will produce an F3 generation.

Now the seedline is stabilizing, and further inbreeding creates F4, F5, and F6 generations.

Knowledge and instinct are vital in breeding for the ideal strain and determining plants that are best suited for the growing conditions and produce the wanted results.

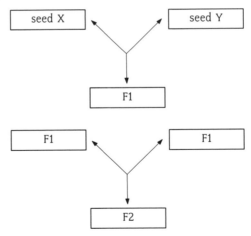

Chart shows the flow towards breeding a stable strain.

Stabilizing Unknown Seeds

If a grower continues to inbreed seeds over successive generations, the plants will become uniform. For example, If two unknown seeds produce a male and a female and reproduce to make seeds; a male and female from those parent plants can be used to make new seeds. Then, a male and female of the latest generation is used to make seeds. In time, consistency will show up.

Experimental Hermaphrodite Results

Plants that have been crossed using a chosen hermaphrodite and a strong genetically different female (without hermaphroditic characteristics) can sometimes be top quality, although the most difficult to make.

Hermaphrodites can look almost entirely female, with only a few male pollen sacks. On the other hand, hermaphrodites can look nearly completely male, with only a few small buds that easily go unnoticed. Or hermaphrodites can look somewhere in between male and female by having a decent supply of male pollen and female buds.

The cross between a female cutting and its mother that was shocked into hermaphroditism creates stability in the seed line, yet can produce a risky supply of hermaphrodite offspring. Seeds made from hermaphroditic pollen can produce more females than crosses from a single male and single female source, in most cases. Generally, self-pollinated hermaphrodites make less female seed and more hermaphrodites than a cross between a hermaphrodite and a non-hermaphroditic female. Hermaphrodites are a touchy issue.

Hermaphroditic breeding results can be different from strain to strain. Female plants that were offspring from hermaphrodite pollen have the potential to turn hermaphroditic when they overmature.

Many growers like to stay a mile away from hermaphroditic crosses because they can be a risk to the seed grower who wants buds without seeds. Since hermaphroditism is often triggered by events such as environmental conditions, hermaphrodites can be time bombs when used anywhere but in a controlled environment. Often though, hermes will only produce the odd pollen sack that will make a seed or so at the plant nodes. Some growers that make female seed will often pick a male and female from that seedlot and inbreed them in order to reduce potential hermaphrodite problems, yet have a supply of consistent seeds.

The question many would ask is, "Why play around with hermaphrodites to achieve a higher female count, when sexing plants and cloning is so easy?"

Making Hermaphrodites from Females

Here is one method for forcing plants to turn hermaphroditic. At harvest time outdoors, a grower can harvest the plant, while making sure to leave some lower vegetation so it can be rejuvenated back into a vegetative state indoors. If this outdoor plant is transplanted from a permanent site to a container, then placed indoors to rejuvenate back with an 18-hour photoperiod, and flowered again at 12 hours when there is plenty of new growth, it may produce seed. It takes about 3 weeks to a month to begin the rejuvenation process. Before the rejuvenation takes place, the plant will look like it has no growth potential. One experiment of this type resulted in four hermaphrodites from four transplants. Clones from such plants will also be hermes.

It is important to always watch for hermaphroditic qualities in all aspects of growing, because hermes can easily go undetected and produce unwanted seed. Some hermaphrodites show female traits throughout early flowering, then suddenly produce unexpected male pollen sacks on the top. With correct timing, it is possible to pull off the unopened pollen sacks so that other females near the plant won't produce seed.

Seed Storage

Mature seeds can be saved and the immature seeds can be discarded. Immature seeds will look white and / or pale green. Mature seeds are brown with black specks. The time when the flowers are picked often affects the quality of seed.

Seeds can be stored in an airtight glass container like a canning jar or a ginseng vial with a rubber stopper. Little vials are nice for the ease of keeping tabs on several varieties. Containers should always be labeled immediately in order to keep accurate records.

Once the seeds are in glass, they can be put in the freezer, wrapped in plastic and buried in the ground, or stored in some other cool, dry, dark place.

Seeds should be stored at least one month before germinating. They can last several years in storage and still have high germination rates. On the other hand, beautiful-looking seeds that have been stored properly can have low germination rates. Germination rates lower as the seeds age, although some strains have longer shelf lives than other ones. In fact, some strains have the ability to have high germinating rates after years of storage at room temperature.

Before seeds are relied on for a crop, it helps to know how well they germinate.

7

Composting

Composting allows a grower to fertilize his buds with food waste. If the food is not composted it is sent to the landfill and helps nobody. But, if it is composted indoors or outside, the result is a ready made plant food. Compost is very easy to use. A grower can add compost to quality dirt and get quality bud.

There are two standard methods types of composting: heated compost and worm composting.

Heated Compost

Making hot compost involves using aerobic bacteria to break down food scraps, etc., and turning it into usable compost. Hot compost can be made in as little as 2 to 8 weeks. The temperature of the compost pile is the key. The temperature of the compost pile can be between 100 and 160°F. A rod can be purchased to determine the temperature, or feeling by hand is an option. Turning the compost regularly and adding materials such as perlite, sawdust, and peat moss helps to add aeration for the bacteria to the pile. When the bacteria thrive, compost breakdown will happen faster.

Hot composting is a good method for an impatient gardener that wants usable compost as soon as possible.

Worm Composting
Making Worm Castings and Organic Matter

Worm composting consists of using worms to consume food scraps, digest dirt and other materials, and then excrete worm castings, which is a rich fertilizer that contains most plant loving elements like nitrogen, trace elements, and humic acids. The key to using worms is to provide them with the proper temperature in the compost (60 to 75°F). The worms will reproduce and be most productive in this range.

When the worms have done their job of making the compost , they should be taken out of the bin and placed in a pile. Then, a light or sunlight should be allowed to shine on the pile. The light will make the worms repel downward into the pile. Now, the compost which contains organic matter and worm castings can be collected from the top portion of the pile. This is a great way to make organic matter and worm castings cheaply, which cost an arm and a leg at the local garden centers.

Composting is good for the environment and plants.

Making a Compost Bin

Bin construction is standard for hot composting or worm composting. A compost bin can be made using five pieces of wood or steel that are 3x3 feet high. A matching lid may be added if a bin is used. Nice, rich-looking, fine black dirt can be layered on the bottom 2 to 8 inches. A well-draining piece of ground (no bin) works too.

Add vegetable, fruit, and seafood scraps that break down relatively easily. Scraps can be blended or put through a food processor to speed up the process.

As soon as the layer of food scraps is 2 to 8 inches high, it should be covered with a 1 to 4-inch dirt layer. If worm composting is the plan, a grower should place a few hundred to a thousand worms (such as Red Wigglers or African Night Crawlers) into the bin. People raise worms, and fisherman supply guys sell them. Adding common earthworms from the yard will work, too, but they are slower to reproduce and will be less thorough eaters. If the soil is already nice and wormy in that location, many more worms will be attracted to the compost pile. This cycle can now go on and on (dirt, then food scraps, then dirt). The worms are added only once.

The worm population will multiply in time, and taking worms from one compost pile and adding them to a new one is an option, so that piles can decompose on a predictable schedule to allow for usable compost in the garden.

It is recommended that you turn the contents of each compost bin with a pitchfork or claw periodically to help speed up the breakdown process and add air to the composted blend. For hot composting, a pile can be turned every day, every few days, or every week. A compost bin or pile can break down completely in two weeks to a few months, depending on the pile temperature and quality of compost pile. The composted material can be made more fertile by adding dolomite lime (one or more cups), up to a bag of manure when the fine dirt is added, and / or the odd dose of cottonseed meal.

Tips: During the cold of winter, a decent layer of straw on top of the pile is needed so the worms will have warmth and will stay in the higher spots of the compost pile to break down new food scraps. The pile should stay moist. It should not be allowed to dry out, but it shouldn't be allowed to become water-logged either.

Underground Outdoor Worm Bin

The underground worm bin a good way to make worm castings because the temperature below the ground surface is warmer than above the ground in cooler conditions, yet, it is cooler in the hot months of summer. Since red worms thrive at 60 to 75°F, this location will help meet those needs.

Typically, a person that raises worms will need to dig trenches, or place wooden boxes into the ground. If a trench is used, the bottom of the trench can be lined with gravel, or 6 mil black plastic with slits cuts into it so that water can drain freely. Each row can be 2 feet wide and 2 feet deep, and any length desired.

If worms are kept outside over the course of a cold winter, a 4-foot deep pit can be dug and covered with insulating material like straw to protect the worms in cold conditions. During the active months of spring, summer and fall, the worm trenches should be covered with plywood to keep out bugs and birds.

The bin needs to be moist, but not soaked. The care for a bin is very little labor. It will not dry out too quickly.

If a grower wants to make a nice dirt mix with worm castings and soil, 50% soil and a 50% bedding mix can be used. The bedding mix can be peat moss and composted manure, or composted manure. After the worms have done their job eating the manure, they will have left their castings in the mix. This mix would work great for growing small plants for top buds.

Under optimum temperature conditions with a decent supply of worms, quality castings can be made in just a few months. As worms multiply, the number of outdoor bins can too.

Indoor Worm Bin

The four main items a vermicompost maker needs are a box, bedding, red wiggler worms, water, and food waste. Any wood or plastic box that is 2-foot by 2-foot and 7 to 9 inches high will work fine. If a plastic tub like a Rubbermaid is used, small holes can be made in the bottom for drainage using a small drill bit or sharp knife. Something should be placed underneath the box to collect the runoff moisture so that it won't stain the floor. If no holes are made in the plastic bin, the bedding must be moist, but not soaked.

An easy bedding mix is probably kicking around the house, such as 70% shredded paper product like corrugated cardboard, newspaper, or letter paper, and 30% peat moss. Since composting is being done with the red wiggler manure worm, the bedding could have any percentage of manure. Some worm raisers feed their worms composted livestock manure to eat up their smelly livestock crap and get back nice, black gold worm castings. If straight manure is used, it should be composted, not fresh and hot. The worm castings may be excrement from the worms, but they do not stink.

A half cup of dirt can be added to the box too so that grit is available for the worms' gizzards.

The whole blend should be mixed thoroughly and moistened with a few gallons of water. Then the worms can be added. The beds should never dry out or become over-saturated because that is not the desired habitat of the red wiggler. The box should be covered because the worms do not like light.

With a 2-foot by 2-foot bin, you should imagine dividing it into 9 equal parts, which would like an Xs and Os game. Every time a small bucket of compost is full in the kitchen, it can be buried into one of the nine equal parts. After filling all nine sites, the process can be repeated so that all of the bedding and garbage is converted into compost.

At this point, all of the product can be used for the plants. Or, half of the compost can be moved into another compost bin while the other half of the bin is filled with new bedding. Now, there are two boxes with compost and fresh bedding. After this new bedding has made new compost, $\frac{1}{2}$ of the castings can be used for the garden and the process can be repeated. Or, this effect can be multiplied and you can have four boxes on the go. When you have enough boxes and sufficient garbage, you can make a continual supply of compost by using half for the garden and the other half as starting material.

Red wigglers require a temperature between 60 to 75°F to be productive eaters and rapidly reproductive. If the area is cold, a thermostatically controlled heat cord can be wrapped around the box to keep the worm bin warm. Some horticulture heat cords are thermostatically controlled at 72°F. Another option is to place a heat pad under a bin that is placed on 2x4s. Heat pads are available at drug stores.

This is small scale compost making, but, it could make enough fertilizing material to grow at least enough bud for personal use. If there is a good supply of composted manure from a farmer, manure can be used in place of food scraps.

Indoor worm bins can be stacked up in a room to make a lot of castings in a small space, if there is enough worms and bedding to make several bins. A person can use fourteen gallon totes, like a Rubbermaid® tote for the bins because they provide enough space and they are easy to lift and stack.

Compost Turners

A ComposTumbler® can be purchased to make compost quickly, and with no mess. These are bins that heat the compost materials up to speed up the breakdown process. They are less than $200, and can be of extreme value in an apartment. A grower could make all his fertilizer with this unit, if a fresh food diet was part of his equation.

You can also build your own compost turner.

Building a Compost Turner

A real cheap method for making an easy to turn bin is to use a garbage can as the source for holding the compost.

Materials

1. Strong plastic garbage can (15 to 40-gallon).
2. Twelve 2-foot pieces of 1 1/2-inch PVC.
3. Eight 1-foot pieces of 1 1/2-inch PVC.
4. Eight 1 1/2-inch PVC elbows.
5. Four 1 1/2-inch PVC Ts.
6. Six eye-hook.s
7. Three bungy cords.

Procedure

A. A hole should be drilled with a 2 to 3-inch holesaw, halfway from the bottom of the can. Now the can should be rotated 180° and another hole drilled at the same height.

B. One of the 2-foot PVC pieces runs through the middle. This will support the can.

C. Another 2-foot piece of PVC runs under the can parallel to the 2-foot piece that runs through the can.

D. All 4 ends of the 2-foot PVC pieces are connected to the PVC Ts.

E. Then the 1-foot lengths are connected to the T-ends.

F. Now the elbows are connected the exposed ends of the 1-foot lengths.

G. Connect the rest of the 2-foot pieces to the rest of the PVC elbows.

H. Now the elbows should be placed to connect the vertical 2-foot PVC pieces to the horizontal 1-foot pieces.

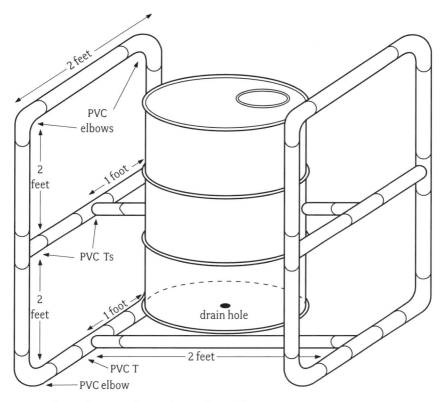

PVC and a garbage can be used to make quick compost.

I. The eye-hooks should inserted evenly around the diameter of the bucket. Bungy cords will be used to secure the lid when the container is flipped over and over to allow for aeration.

J. Finally, drill a 1-inch hole at the bottom of the can to allow for drainage.

This bin can now be used for hot composting or worm composting. For hot composting, it should be rotated frequently, such as every day, every few days, or once a week.

8

Troubleshooting

General Outdoor Cultivation Problems
Causes and Remedies
Problem: Plants turn yellow at any time during all growth phases, less the final 2 weeks until harvest.

Cause: Lack of light or nutrition.

Remedy:

1. Outdoor container plants should be moved into full sun. Competing vegetation should be cleared out. If the weather has been miserable, hoping for a change is the only option.

Light levels must be extremely low for this to occur, because most plants will stay green and use less nutrients if grown in shady areas. Strain type is key.

2. Hopefully, the pH of soil or nutrient solution is proper.

For nutrition problems, plants should be fed with a balanced nutrient formulation as explained in this guide, or the medium should be flushed well. After the medium is cleaned, a grower should add a proper nutrient formulation.

This is the best way to deal with nutritional problems because it is very difficult to isolate one deficiency from another. Also, salts locked up in the soil may be inhibiting the plant from getting what it needs because nutrients are locked up, even when an ample supply of nutrients already exist in a growing medium such as soil / soilless mix.

Again, if the plants are fed properly, the pH is good, and the medium is not over-toxified, then a complete diet will be in the plants' best interest.

The top leaves and new leaves should always be watched to see the color. The old leaves may not green up. Old leaves will reach a point of yellowness, and cannot turn around. Nitrogen is a common deficiency that first hits the older leaves. If the leaves are yellowing just slightly, then they should revive to a green color in less than a week.

Problem: Burning shoots.
Cause: Overfertilization.
Remedy: For overfertilization, a grower should flush each plant with several gallons of plain water immediately. The runoff (water that is flushed through medium) should be 0PPM. Feeding can be resumed a few days later.

Problem: Clones dry up and look near death.
Cause: Lid was not placed properly on the flat or it has holes in it, plants may not have been misted at regular intervals, or the heat pad thermostat may be malfunctioning. Or the rooting medium has dried up.
Remedy: Regular mistings and close attention and careful monitoring are necessary so that the rooting medium stays moist. If the clones are severely wilted new clones should be cut. Heat pad with high temperatures can dry out cloning mediums very quickly.

Problem: Germinated seedlings didn't sprout through the mix, although everything was done as instructed in chapter 1.
Cause: Mice dug in mix and ate fresh shoots.
Remedy: The nursery room should be made so that mice cannot enter. Surrounding lights and plants with wood or plastic will prevent access.

Problem: Seedlings grew tall and spindly and are flopping over.
Cause: Light levels are not sufficient: fluorescents are too high above the plants or outside conditions were extremely poor. Enough gray and dark days and the plant will stretch for light, no matter how good the food supply is.
Remedy: The seedlings should be transplanted to larger pots and the stalks should be buried up to their first set of leaves. New roots will form from out of the stalks.

Problem: Fertilizer bags were broken into.
Cause: Rats like several types of organic fertilizers, such as canola meal and Flower Power.
Remedy: Fertilizers should be stored in a totally enclosed area.

Problem: Some plant leaves have many holes, with or without bugs present.
Cause: Bugs, or disease. Certain strains have these problems more than others.
Remedy: For bugs, Nitrozyme® (Growth Plus™) with organic insecticidal soap may be used as spelled out on pages 117 to 120. The right hours for foliar feeding are soon before or after the lights turn on indoors, or in the morning or early evening for outdoor plants.

Leaf spot fungus may show up in the outdoors whether or not the mix is contaminated. The inner parts of the leaves begin to rust, then the material falls out and leaves holes. A grower should get to the root of the problem by using 35% hydrogen peroxide (1 to 5ml per gallon) when watering, and using calcium peroxide (i.e. Soil blaster) or 35% hydrogen peroxide (2 to 5ml per gallon) before reusing soilless mix / soil. Leaf spot fungus problems are unpredictable. It will attack weak or healthy-looking plants. For example, in a 6 plant garden, one or more may have the disease, while the others will show no signs at all. This is not an epidemic.

Problem: Outdoor plants look abnormal in growth from others that are treated the same.
Cause: Predators such as slugs or deer. Or a frost could mutate the plants.
Remedy: The first step is to figure out what the predator is. Looking for the predator or a sign, such as slug slime, or deer footprints will determine the predator. Then it is recommended to use one of the control methods described on pages 117 to 122.

For a frost mutation, a grower should have a backup supply of plants because the mutated one may or may not grow or flower properly.

Problem: Outdoor plant fell over.
Cause: Too much mass combined with nature's elements like wind and rain.
Remedy: Plants should be properly pruned and bent as discussed on pages 112 to 116.

Problem: Outdoor plants grew tall, but produced very few flowers.
Cause: Competing vegetation in the area blocked out sun to the lower parts of the plant and therefore only the top sections produced; lack of bloom food; too small a container size; or a poor strain for the area.
Remedy:
1. Pruning out surrounding vegetation with shears will allow a plant to receive full sun without blockage.
2. The right strain should always be used.
3. A proper fertilizing formula should be used, such as one of those described in chapter 3.

Problem: Outdoor flowers did not finish blooming, although good money was paid for an expensive mix.
Cause: Poor flowering conditions and/or wrong strain.
Remedy:
1. Using the right strain(s) with new fertilizers the next time is a step forward. Growing the right plants is half the battle. A plant's ability to grow in a robust manner and produce the type of flower preferred is more genetic than a matter of technique. For example, a novice grower who grows small, underfertilized buds can produce buds of equal quality to a master gardener. A master can only do so much in terms of quality (not quantity) with a specific plant, no matter what.
2. Plants where no care is taken can acquire too many problems to list, but here are a few: Lack of water to a plant or overwatering a plant can stunt its growth.

Spraying an overdose of insecticide an put a plant on the path to non recovery. Transplanting a plant in the flowering state while mangling the roots can shut down performance levels. Overfertilizing a plant can retard growth performance.

Glossary

Acidic A solution or soil is acidic when the pH is less than 7.0.

Aeroponics A growing system in which plant roots are fed with a misted solution. An aeroponic system is similar to a misting system that is used in a supermarket to spray vegetables.

Alkaline A solution or soil is alkaline when the pH is greater than 7.0.

Breeding Making seeds from male pollen and female pistils.

Budding The process of producing flowers.

Clone A new plant that has the same genetic make up as the mother plant.

Cloning Making an identical genetic copy of the mother plant.

Composting Recycling household waste in order to make fertilizer.

Cutting see *clone*

Feeding Giving plants their desired plant food.

Flowering The process of producing flowers.

Flooding and Draining Feeding plant roots with a solution that floods a table, then drains back into a reservoir.

Flushing Removing salts from a growing medium. Flushing is also a process of removing elements from the leaves and flowers too.

Germinating Bringing a seed to life.

Hermaphrodites Plants that have both male and female reproductive parts.

Humidity It is a measurement of the percentage of moisture that is in the air.

Hydroponics Feeding plants with a nutrient solution in a medium that does not contain soil.

Medium The material a plant is grown in, such as soilless mix, perlite, rockwool, and coconut fibers.

Organic Naturally occuring fertilizers.

Parts per million (PPM) This is the amount of 1 part of something in a million parts of another. In terms of fertilizer, 1,500PPM means there are 1,500 parts of fertilizer in 1,000,000 parts of water.

pH The acidity of a solution. 7.0 is neutral, <7.0 is acidic and >7.0 is alkaline.

Pistil The female reproductive organ.

Pollen The fertilizing element of a flowering plant.

Predator Another living organism that targets the plant in order to feed and often weakens or kills it in the process.

Pruning Removing top and side shoots in order to produce a bushier plant.

Rejuvenating Bringing a harvested plant back into vegetative growth.

Reservoir The tank that holds nutrient solution in a hydroponic/aeroponic system.

Rooting The process of a clone forming new roots.

Seedlings Young plants that were started from seed. The seedling phase lasts somewhere near 5 weeks before the plants grow at a fast rate.

Sexing Forcing a seedling to show it reproductive organs.

Shoots The new plant growth that extends from branches.

Soilless mix A growing medium that is mainly composed of peat moss, perlite, and lime.

Strain A variety of cannabis, such as Timewarp and Blueberry.

Sweating Drawing moisture from the stalks of dried flowers.

Top-feeding Applying a nutrient solution from the top of the growing medium.

Training Positioning limbs with string, plant yo-yos, etc., in order to allow the plant to receive more light.

Transplanting Moving plants into a new medium.

Vegetative growth The growth phase before plants produce buds.

Index

Also available from Green Candy Press

Marijuana New School Indoor by Jeff Mowta

This comprehensive book provides step-by-step instructions for 20 affordable indoor growing setups. Packed with over 600 illustrations and photos, the book walks readers through the construction of both hydroponic and soil systems and shows how to maintain them throughout the growing season. Everything the budding gardener needs to know is covered in astonishing detail, including setting up a starter room, cloning, indoor designs, harvesting, drying, storing, troubleshooting, breeding, composting, as well as the latest tips and techniques. $19.95

Available from www.greencandypress.com

Also available from Green Candy Press

Marijuana Cooking:
Good Medicine Made Easy
by Bliss Cameron and
Veronica Greene

Bliss Cameron and Veronica Green guide would-be chefs through the process of making their own tasty and healthy home remedies using marijuana as the main ingredient. Step-by-step, high quality photographs  grace nearly every page, walking readers through the creation of such recipes as recipes Bliss Balls, Butterscotch Blondies, and Honey Chocolate Brownies. $14.95

The Good Bud Guide
by Albie

Designed like a guide to fine wines, this handy book itemizes and profiles a wide range of marijuana strains, each one accompanied by an educated evaluation of its aroma, taste, and effect. High-quality glossy images and precise growing information help discerning enthusiasts identify the best-bred bud and perhaps even grow their own. The most comprehensive strain guide every produced. $19.95

Cannabis Breeder's Bible
by Greg Green

This groundbreaking guide to breeding covers all the inside dope: new hybridization techniques, international seed law issues, protecting new breeds or strains from knockoff artists, shipping seeds and clones, breeding lab designs, product testing, primordial cannabis, landrace and lost strains, common mutations, and more. $21.95

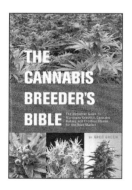

Available from www.greencandypress.com